DESIGN
RULES

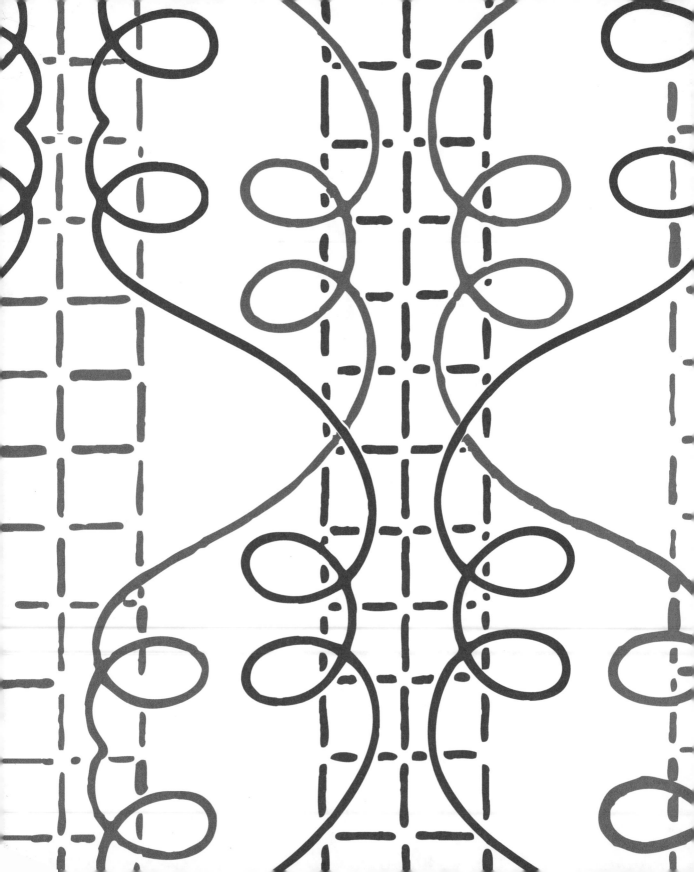

DESIGN RULES

THE INSIDER'S GUIDE TO BECOMING YOUR OWN DECORATOR

ELAINE GRIFFIN

GOTHAM BOOKS

GOTHAM BOOKS
Published by Penguin Group (USA) Inc.
375 Hudson Street, New York, New York 10014, U.S.A.
Penguin Group (Canada), 90 Eglinton Avenue East, Suite 700, Toronto, Ontario M4P 2Y3, Canada (a division
of Pearson Penguin Canada Inc.); Penguin Books Ltd, 80 Strand, London WC2R 0RL, England; Penguin Ireland,
25 St Stephen's Green, Dublin 2, Ireland (a division of Penguin Books Ltd); Penguin Group (Australia), 250
Camberwell Road, Camberwell, Victoria 3124, Australia (a division of Pearson Australia Group Pty Ltd); Penguin
Books India Pvt Ltd, 11 Community Centre, Panchsheel Park, New Delhi—110 017, India; Penguin Group (NZ), 67
Apollo Drive, Rosedale, North Shore 0632, New Zealand (a division of Pearson New Zealand Ltd); Penguin Books
(South Africa) (Pty) Ltd, 24 Sturdee Avenue, Rosebank, Johannesburg 2196, South Africa

Penguin Books Ltd, Registered Offices: 80 Strand, London WC2R 0RL, England

Published by Gotham Books, a member of Penguin Group (USA) Inc.

First printing, November 2009
1 3 5 7 9 10 8 6 4 2

"Grille Moderne" is a hand-printed wallpaper by Studio Printworks

Gotham Books and the skyscraper logo are trademarks of Penguin Group (USA) Inc.

LIBRARY OF CONGRESS CATALOGING-IN-PUBLICATION DATA
Griffin, Elaine (Elaine Joaquina)
Design rules : the insider's guide to becoming your own decorator / by Elaine Griffin.—1st ed.
p.   cm.
Ch. 1. Living rooms—Ch. 2. Dining rooms—Ch. 3. Bedrooms—Ch. 4. Powder rooms—Ch. 5. Kitchens—
Ch. 6. Bathrooms—Ch. 7. Foyers and Entryways—Ch. 8. Basements—Ch. 9. Laundry rooms—
Ch. 10. Window treatments—Ch. 11. Floors—Ch. 12. Color.
ISBN 978-1-592-40506-0 (pbk. original) 1. Interior decoration.   I. Title
NK2110.G75   2009
747—dc22   2009017730

Printed in the United States of America
Set in Mrs. Eaves
Designed by Chris Welch

While the author has made every effort to provide accurate telephone numbers and Internet addresses at the time of
publication, neither the publisher nor the author assumes any responsibility for errors, or for changes that occur
after publication. Further, the publisher does not have any control over and does not assume any responsibility for
author or third-party Web sites or their content.

FOR MOM, MY ORIGINAL STYLE GURU,

AND MICHAEL, MY TRUEST INSPIRATION

CONTENTS

ACKNOWLEDGMENTS

Fashion fades, but style is eternal! And so are all the *maaaah-velous* people who helped *Design Rules* come to be: Janis Donnaud, Agent Extraordinaire; Lucia Watson, the World's Most Patient Editor (who will soon be gray overnight because I am the world's worst procrastinator); Megan Newman, Style Personified; Kathleen Hackett, writing partner de rêve; Mim Silverstein, Miss Numbers; John Burgoyne, our own Picasso; and Temo Callahan, whose Studio Printworks *Grille Moderne* wallpaper has been adapted for use in our interior book design.

It's been more than a decade in design for me now, so I'll add a Texas-style bow (post-deb, at my age, doll, and my knees can barely make it to the floor!) with deepest gratitude to the industry icons for whose support your Designer Girlfriend here is eternally indebted: James P. Druckman, Margaret Russell, Adrian Kahan Leibowitz, Marianne Rohrlich, Karen Carroll and Lydia Somerville, Peter Marino, Scott Salvator and Michael Zabriskie, Samantha Nestor, Irene Wilson, Janice Langrall, O.W., Gayle King, Amy Gross, Suzanne Slesin, and Adam Glassman from the *O at Home* days, and the hardworking trustees of the Kips Bay Showhouse. Massive, massive smooches to all the editors, vendors, contractors, tradespeople, clients, and assistants who have shared laughter, décor, and fabulosity with me daily since 1997. Love, endlessly, as always, to Mom and Michael.

XOXO—
Elaine

DESIGN RULES

INTRODUCTION

As an established interior designer, I thought, quite frankly, I was the cat's meow. I imagined ladies all over the country wistfully longing to engage my services. I just knew they secretly coveted my counsel, wishing for the payday that would allow them to have me come work my mojo on their manses. Who on earth, reasoned I, would want to tackle the thankless task of decorating their own home when they could hire an *expert* to magically transform it into an Oasis of Paradise in the mere twinkling of an eye? Surely a winning lottery ticket was the only thing keeping us apart.

Darling, how *wrong* I was! *Nothing could have been further from the truth!*

Newsflash! American Society of Interior Designers (ASID) polls indicate that most (49 percent!) American homeowners prefer to handle their own decorating—only 14 percent of them used an interior designer's services, whether on a beer or champagne budget.

The more I thought about it, the more sense it all made: You want your home to look like you and nobody else, you take pride in where you live and how *faaabulous* it looks, nothing feels better than saying, "I did it all myself!" when it's finished, and who *wouldn't* want to save on all those fees decorators (have to, to be fair) charge?

So I got with the program, picked up a pen, and set out to put to paper some of the practical decorating standards and timeless rules that are second nature to the design professionals who implement them daily, but ones that most folks don't know about. These are the design truths that transcend style, era, and aesthetic; the tips, proportions, and trade secrets that will help you create flowing, balanced, warm, and great-looking rooms that are delights to behold and to be in, whatever decorative style you favor.

It's the secret stuff your decorator would have told you if you were hiring one; the design musts without which you can't successfully do a room but don't want to pay a pro to learn about, either. They're the questions that people who *do* use a designer ask, too. All for the price of the book! Honey, *What! A! Bargain!*

I've made it all shamelessly simple (*whew!*), and packed *Design Rules* with the information that knowledge-seeking do-it-yourself designers of both sexes shouldn't live without, wherever a sofa meets a chair. If you have an idea of how you want your space to *feel* when it's finished, but aren't *quiiiiiiiiite* sure how to get there, then, sugar, *this* is the book for *you*!

We'll go room-by-room throughout your entire house and show you *exactly* what you need to know in order for everything to flow and be visually successful. We'll attack furniture placement, size, and layout; color, lighting, window treatments, painting, flooring, cabinetry, materials, finishes, specific proportions and dimensions, and, *of course,* accessories, darling! We'll cover everything you need to know about decorating . . . *and* have a giggle or two while we're at it, because as Dorothy Draper once famously said, *"Decorating Is Fun!"*

So let's get started.

SPACES YOU LIVE IN

LIVING ROOMS, FAMILY ROOMS, GREAT ROOMS, AND DENS

The living room, family room, great room, and den are the hardest-working spaces of your house. They're the rooms you spend the most time in, and they get the greatest wear and tear. Whether you are a studio apartment dweller or are gifted with a sprawling suburban domain, the design rules for the public spaces are the same. Identify the elements that work for your particular space, scale them to suit its size, then thoughtfully devise a floor plan for maximum comfort. Whether you dress them in soothing Zen style or opt for boldly colored decorative drama, they're high-performance places that need, designwise, to deliver.

THE LAYOUT

When planning where to put your furniture, remember that nine times out of ten, the whole point of seating is for people to sit and talk to each other. Think in terms of *conversation groups* and not just seating groups—chairs should be close enough to the sofa and each other for people to talk comfortably and intimately. Five fabulous seating group setups are shown on the opposite page.

Also take into consideration how you like to live and entertain. Is your home Clubhouse Central for all your friends and family? Then try to accommodate as many people as you sensibly can in your space. Scatter pull-up seating options creatively throughout the room: benches, stools, and odd chairs placed symmetrically against walls (more on this below). At the very least, plan to have seating for a party of four, even if you are an antisocial hermit living in a studio. (Honey, you never know who'll drop by one day!)

Keep in mind that arranging a pair of sofas facing each other looks great in a photo but is always awkward for conversation in real life, because the only time people sit directly across from each other (while not dining) is for formal interviews. Otherwise we turn and talk to the person sitting beside us. If you're doing the two-sofas-plus-a-pair-of-armchairs setup, position the sofas at a right angle to each other and the chairs across from one of the sofas. That'll work best to create warmth and intimacy in your room.

It's best to find the focal point of a room, and then arrange furniture in a square or a rectangle, either facing or in front of that focal point. What is a focal point, you ask? It's easier to think of "orientation" rather than "focal point"—after all,

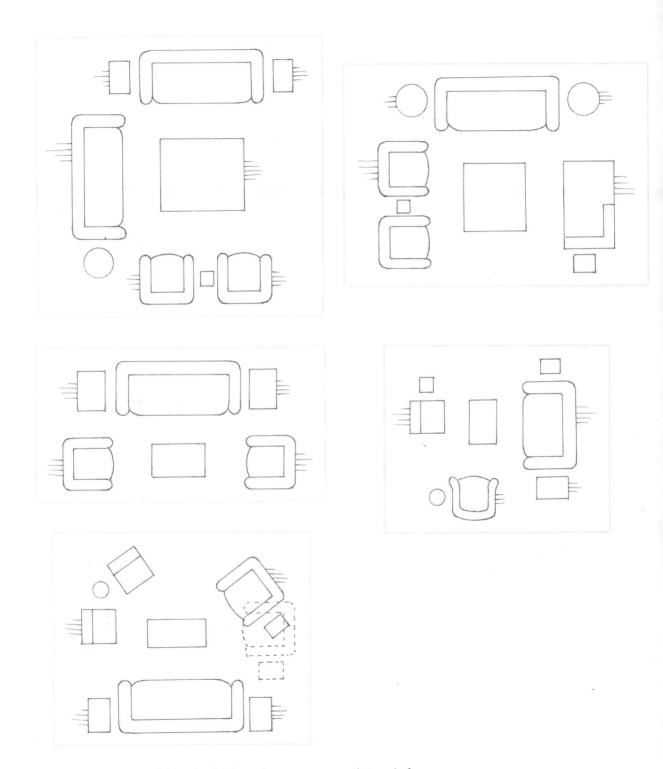

Mix and match any of these five fab floor plans to create one that works for you.

the furniture is "oriented" around it, not focused on it. That said, a fireplace is always the focal point of its room. Other good bets for fireplace-less rooms:

- In front of a bay window or a plate-glass picture window
- Opposite an arched entrance
- On a wall between symmetrical sets of windows
- The longest wall
- The shortest wall—create a focal point with a folding screen

TRADE SECRET

Always pay attention to the wall space directly across the room from doors. This is also true for the vistas at the end of corridors, at the top of the stairs, and on landings. Create an eye-catching visual destination with something as simple as a mirror or piece of art hung on the wall, with an odd chair ("*odd chairs*" are desk- or dining-size one-offs, like you might find at a flea market, and not part of a set) sitting below. ✳

Use a divided or pair of folding screens to create a focal point in a featureless room.

If you have an oversize living room, set up several conversation groupings. A lone sofa and pair of chairs will look lost in the vastness. Hotel lobbies are great inspiration for setting up seating groups (but only inspiration—sugar, you don't want your living room to be that impersonal). It's really about breaking a larger space into zones.

Rule of Thumb

In any layout, remember that you need a minimum of 26 to 36 inches clear as a pathway to cross through the room without bumping into anything. Make that 36 to 48 inches if you like it airy.

Don't be afraid to float your seating group in the center of the room, especially when highlighting a fireplace. For this to work, you'll need a minimum of 29 inches left clear for passage. If you have at least 4 feet of clear space between the edge of the sofa and the opposite wall, put a long bench, low bookcase, or several benches along that wall for pull-up seating or display options (all the more if you live down South, where we just love to pull up a chair and sit a spell). If you have 5 feet or more of clear space, put a sofa or settee (*settees* are basically long, framed chairs, with or without cushions, that can be as long as sofas but are always shallower) against the empty wall to create another conversation group. (Skip the coffee table; you most likely won't have enough room to walk by. But add a diminutive one, if you do! Set up side tables on either side of the settee for drinks and lamps.)

In a long, narrow room, try putting the sofa on the shortest

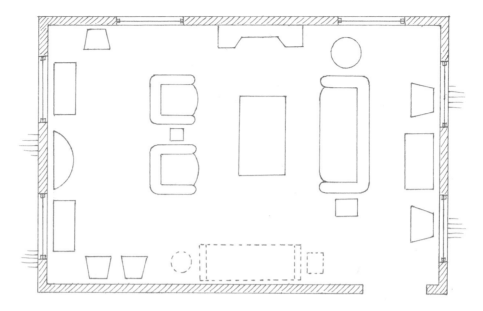

Float your seating group in the center of the room, especially around a fireplace.

wall, which is especially pretty in front of windows. (This doesn't work if you're floating furniture in the center of the room, since you won't be able to walk around it.) I'm wild about this trick for city dwellers with bite-size living rooms, especially using either a 60-inch-long loveseat or a 72- to 76-inch-long "city sofa," which still leaves enough room for a cute pair of itty-bitty side tables. Dahling, let your wall length dictate your sofa length in a little living room, and not vice versa.

Open Up Your Space with a Faux Foyer

If you walk straight into your living room from the street, creating a faux foyer will do wonders for your space—the psy-

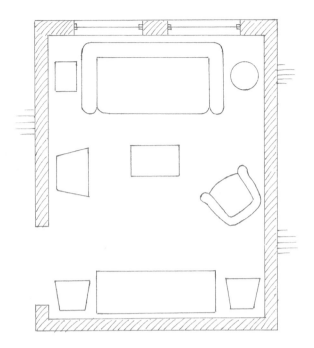

In a tiny room, station the sofa on the shortest wall, not the longest.

chological effect of being one step removed from the Great Outdoors will make your house seem larger. A folding screen extending into the room perpendicular to the door does the trick perfectly. If you have enough space, station a narrow console in front of the screen as a "hall" table to put mail and keys on. (Don't forget your tabletop display with the tray, the flower, and the candle, sugar—you want your tabletops to be *cute*!) The screen should be as tall as possible—you're basically creating a fake wall. See-through Chinese fretwork screens are great. If it's a plain solid screen, decorate both sides of it, since you'll see the back from the living room. (To hang art on the back of a hollow screen, wrap florist's wire or mono-filament line around a nail driven into the top edge of the screen.)

Use a folding screen to create a faux foyer.

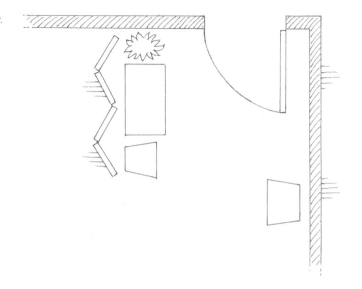

The eye should have something pretty to rest upon as you enter a room.

Create Groupings with Area Rugs

Area rugs are meant to visually anchor the seating group they sit under. This means all four legs of every piece of furniture in the same zone should sit on the rug that's underneath them. Exception: The sofa's rear legs may be off-rug if the sofa is against a wall, but otherwise don't stint on the rug size.

Design Tip

To create a perfectly sized area rug without breaking the bank, have regular carpeting cut to the exact size you need and the edges bound or serged (*serging* is finishing the edges with wool or nylon yarn).

If you're covering the entire room with one area rug, leave 12 to 18 inches clear all around to the wall. In smaller rooms, 7 to 12 inches does the trick. Putting a too-large rug in your small room will stifle the space and make it look even smaller (this is true for any room in the house!).

On the other hand, if you're going for a modern look, *smaller* rugs actually work. It is always lovely to see more of the floor in modern rooms. Not too tiny, though, or little rugs can look jarringly out of proportion with the seating group they anchor, which looks really, really cheesy. In traditional spaces, layering antique (real or faux) Orientals and kilims on top of a seating group-size or room-size sisal or jute rug adds oodles of warmth. *This* is the one time you can get away with using smallish-size rugs (*only! on! top!*), since the bottom rug visually carries the load.

Other Layout Tips

- Folding screens do wonders to take up extra space while simultaneously looking fabulous in supersize rooms. Stand one in a corner (it's okay to pull it out from the wall a couple of feet), and put a round table with a lamp in front of it. An upholstered reading chair with a floor lamp and a tiny mini-table look terrific in front, too.
- Desks look great stationed perpendicular to the wall, not just parallel to it. This is especially true in front of a window, and you can look outside while you work (turn your head, darling).

SIZE AND SHAPE MATTERS

Consoles

Consoles (tall, narrow tables) are among the most versatile pieces of furniture out there. Place a pair of low benches, upholstered ottomans, or 18-inch cubes stylishly underneath a console for use as pull-up seating. Paired chairs flanking a console also work well (but don't do both at once). Almost anytime you have 6 to 8 linear feet of empty space free, it's a perfect spot for a console-pair-of-flanking-chairs combo. It's one of the most useful fillers visually, and you can always pull up the chairs when you need more seating elsewhere in the room. Sit a pretty tray on top of the table, with magazines, an orchid plant, and a fragrant candle. Add a lamp, or a pair of lamps, depending on the size of the table (they shouldn't dominate the tabletop surface), and you're done.

When you're floating a seating group in the middle of the

room, a console table behind the sofa (the two should touch) gives the eye something other than a barren sofa back to look at. The table should not tower over the top of the sofa's back (ideally it should be several inches lower, so whatever you put on the tabletop won't tower over, either); if your table isn't expensive, cut the legs down accordingly. To visually fill the empty space under the console, put a pair of benches or a giant arrangement of greenery in a long, rectangular planter (two smaller ones will also do the trick). Add lamps on top of the table (you'll need an electrical outlet in the floor to plug it in, which an electrician can install), or a pair of tall candles in hurricanes if plug-less. If there's room, add a pair of twin decorative objects on the floor on either side (maybe ceramic sculpture that's just under sofa height, tall twin topiaries, or dainty, diminutive chairs that are too fragile to actually sit in but were just too darned cute to leave in the store).

If you station sofas back-to-back, put a console between the two with a pair of lamps on top for reading light and to vary the height of the objects in the room.

End Tables and Chair Tables

End tables should never loom over the sofa they're next to—they look best just below the arm height. Most sofa arms are 24 inches high, so look for a 22-inch-tall table. Exception: If you have odd tables (i.e., an unmatched pair) and one will be near a corner when it's positioned next to the sofa, that one won't look strange if it's taller than the arm; just make sure it's not taller than the height of the sofa's back. Ditto for a round table. Another exception: If you're standing a *very* tall piece like a highboy or secretary next to your sofa, ignore

Highboys adjacent to sofas break the "low side table" rule.

this rule altogether. Just make sure your sofa zone looks balanced when you're looking at the ensemble together from left to right. If necessary, create a similar height with art on the other side of the sofa to visually balance the tallness of the highboy. P.S.: The tall piece of furniture almost always looks better when it is closer to the corner, so try it out on that side of the sofa first.

Beside every chair there should be a surface such as a small table, stool, or bench that can hold a book, a pen, or a drink. The table should be proportionate to the chair next to it (the smaller the chair, the smaller the table) and always lower than the chair's arm height. Think small and low-ish: 9 by 12-inch mini-tables look great. Ceramic garden stools are fabulous for this, too, along with little Asian-inspired bamboo *tabourets* (that's French for a very small table).

Always sit a tiny table next to an armchair.

Coffee Tables

The most important thing to know about the size of your coffee table is that it should be proportionate either to the room it's in or the furniture grouping it's anchoring. You want to be able to walk around all four sides comfortably. In a small grouping, 15 by 24 inches or smaller can be a great size for a coffee table. Be creative—it doesn't have to be *sold* as a "coffee table" to be one; it's the size that matters most. Consider a pair of 16-inch square or round tea tables, *tabourets*, or even stools or benches in front of smaller sofas or loveseats. If you need a super-size c.t. and can't find one for the life of you, double up on one at the correct length—it's a great look that creatively solves your problem. Upholstered ottomans make adorable coffee tables, particularly for children to wallow on and for adults to prop up their feet. Sit a tray—or two on big ottomans—on the soft top to hold drinks, snacks, and magazines.

In terms of height, whatever you use as your coffee table should always be an inch or two less than the height of the sofa's seat cushion (measure from the floor to the top of the seat cushion). Not clearly seeing the top line of the seat cushion is visually jarring—honey, don't ask me why, but it is. As a rule, the ideal height for most coffee tables is 17 to 18 inches.

If the overall shape of your seating group is square, then your coffee table should be, too. If it's rectangular, then choose a rectangular one, or a pair of small squares that will become a rectangle when you sit them next to each other with 3 inches or so in between. Circular coffee tables correspond to square spaces; ovals to rectangular ones.

The top of your coffee table should always be lower than that of the sofa.

Standard Sizes

Sofas	
Side/End Tables	20 x 36 x 20
	20 x 20 x 18
	18 x 18 (round)
	18 x 26 (round)
Coffee Tables	36 x 24 x 18
	36 x 36 x 18
	36 x 18 (round)
Cubed Stools	18 x 18 x 18
Consoles	48 x 20 x 33

THE COVER-UP: STYLE AND EFFECT

The biggest thing to keep in mind when styling your living room is that between your walls, floors, ceiling, and furniture, only one element can be the star performer in any given room, or your space will look like Dolly Parton's Christmas tree . . . wearing a Halloween costume. Choose which one you'd like to be the dramatic soloist, and make it the boldest/brightest/largest/most patterned. Assign complementary supporting roles to the rest of the cast.

The Rules for Mixing Furniture

- Pay attention to the shapes of the *arms* on your big upholstered pieces in one room. They should relate to each other: all round and curvy arms, or all square or squarish. Round and squarish arms don't mix well and are visually unsettling together.

- Use the "similar shape" rule when mixing furniture from different periods together in one room, too. All clean-lined furniture with similar legs works together (Louis XVI with Art Deco). All furniture with curvy edges or legs works together (Victorian and Louis XIV). All furniture with organic shapes (i.e., Danish modern with Japanese) does, too. Neoclassical goes with Neoclassical (i.e., Federal with Louis XVI), modern with modern (Robsjohn-Gibbings with Heywood-Wakefield) . . . as long as there's a consistent curvy or straight theme going through the bunch. Make a point of adding geometric contrast in your accessories: In a straight-lined room, for example, display several curvy objects on your tabletops and a bouquet of super-fluffy flowers such as peonies.

- All colors of wood can go together in a single space, just like they do in the forest. But avoid having ALL the same color wood in one room; break up the monotony with a painted, gilded, or a different-stained piece or two.

- Don't overupholster. Sofas look great next to upholstered armchairs, true, but they also look great with settees (a settee is a wood-framed seating unit, typically about 60 inches long and not too deep) or wood-framed armchairs. Pair a settee or loveseat (2 feet shorter than a sofa) with dining-size chairs or slipper chairs in a tiny apartment or for a small seating group in a big room.

- Combine skirted and exposed-leg pieces for your seating in a traditional room so it doesn't look "leggy." In modern rooms, however, opting for mostly exposed-leg pieces looks cleaner and more contemporary.

Upholstery and Cushion Rules

- Again, upholstering all your furniture in the same fabric is a design no-no. But *do* use the same fabric for matched pairs of sofas, armchairs, or odd chairs, which unites them visually. Or you can create a "set" of faux matched armchairs using unidentical twins—putting the same fabric on both chairs fools the eye into thinking they're really a set.

- If you need high-performance upholstery fabrics that can stand up to small children, pets, and visiting fraternity brother friends, don't sacrifice style for substance. Indoor/outdoor acrylic fabrics are just what the doctor ordered. (Sunbrella is one brand name, but everyone has them now; the technical name for this fabric is "solution-dyed acrylic.") Ultrasuede—or any synthetic suede (look for "polyester" on the content label)—spot-cleans magnificently with dishwashing liquid on a damp sponge and is virtually indestructible, as are leather and vinyl. Microfiber, a lighter weight sueded polyester, is next on the list for durability, but opt for the sturdier ultra-suede if you can.

- Choose down-wrapped foam inserts for your sofa and armchair seat cushions. Yes, pure down filling is the ultimate in luxury, but I assure you the daily plumping that down cushions require will send you to the mad-house in *no time flat.* All-foam inserts look cheesy and are uncomfortable to sit on. Foam centers, sandwiched between fluffy muslin envelopes of down and feathers, are the prettiest to look at and loveliest to sit upon. From there you can vary the density to soft, medium, or hard-feeling cushions to your liking if you're having custom upholstery done.

- When your sofa starts to sag and look forlorn, it's not necessary to buy a whole new unit: Change the cushion inserts, which is never a pricey operation. Take them to an upholsterer and ask for new inserts to be fabricated.

- Mix up the textures of the materials, finishes, and textures in a room for contrast and visual balance: shiny + matte, rough + sleek, nubby + smooth, dark + light, and plain + patterned. Choose bright, patterned throw pillows for a dark, solid color sofa.

- Always, always, *always* sit your dark sofa on a lighter rug. And vice versa. Contrast creates coziness.

LIGHT THE WAY

More so than in any other room in the house, lamps rule in the living room. I am diametrically opposed to overhead lighting in living rooms, dens, and great rooms, unless it's recessed and *discreet*. If you have a dining table or one of those cute little billiards tables in there, a chandelier or billiards lamp is fine above that, but otherwise, sugar, *let lamplight rule!* As should dimmers, too: Go to your local hardware store and buy as many as there are light sources in your living room. Then install one on each. *Every* lighting source in the living room should be on a dimmer for the ultimate in mood control. I'm also a fan of varying the wattage of light bulbs in lamps throughout the room, to get the *effect* of dimmers without the garish light dimmed lights can sometimes emit. *Extra credit:* Hardware stores also sell dimmers for *lamps!*

Table and Floor Lamps

- Each of the four corners of the room should be lit by a table or floor lamp. This doesn't mean that they have to be smack dab in the corner, but in the general zone. The object is to avoid dark spots at all costs.
- Every armchair and/or reading chair should have a floor or table lamp near it. Floor lamps are ideal in spaces where there's not enough room for a table to put a lamp on. If your sofa is in a niche just wide enough to accommodate it, position a pair of floor lamps on either side of it (or see swing arm lamps, page 20).
- Vary the scale of the lamps in your room: You want a beefier lamp next to the larger pieces of upholstered furniture.

Bigger lamps draw the eye in first, so put them where you want to focus attention, which is usually adjacent to the sofa (which, in turn, is almost always the largest piece of furniture in the room).

- Paired lamps look great on credenzas and sofa tables, with one placed on either end. The key is to choose a size that relates, scalewise, to the piece of furniture they're on. They rarely look attractive centered on a long table. If you're not using a pair, put a single one off to one end, then balance out the other end with an object that is somewhat smaller in scale just to give that end of the table visual weight.

- Lamps do not have to be identical when flanking the sofa, but they should be of similar proportions. Unify unlike styles with shades in similar colors or shapes.

- If you float your furniture in the center of the room—around the fireplace, for example—have your electrician install floor receptacle outlets to accommodate them. The alternative, running electrical cords under rugs, is a fire hazard, and your Designer Girlfriend here *can't have that*, honey.

Sconces, Swing Arm Lamps, and Picture Lights

Think sconces in places that are awkward to illuminate (i.e., over the fireplace, in a *suuuuupertight* niche, in which case they should be mounted on the short walls) or to simply adorn a vast stretch of wall. They're also great over a seating area—mounted at least 3 to 4 inches above the back of the sofa (more if you're using them to visually "fill" the space) and at least a couple of inches past the upper corners of the sofa's back.

If reading is your favorite thing to do on your sofa, use

swing arm lamps to light the space. They're handsome, but more important, adjustable. Mount them as you would sconces, making sure the bottom of the fixture clears the top of the sofa and are positioned at least 3 to 4 inches beyond the sofa's top edges.

I love picture lights—but not necessarily mounted over art work. They're great affixed to the crown of a bookcase to softly illuminate the spines of the books and also the bookcase's location (fabulous in a hallway!). Picture lights can be hardwired into the wall by boring a hole just below the crown of the case and running the wire through the unit to the wall behind, or cheat by running the wires down the back of the bookcase and plugging them into adjacent outlets.

Overhead Lighting

Now y'all already know how I feel about light shining down from on high in the living room. Not even renters should dwell in a living room with an overhead fixture! If you happen to be one and are stuck with an unattractive overhead fixture, call an electrician immediately and have him or her remove it and install a flat round plate over the opening. That way you can put the fixture back when you move.

Nonetheless, there are exceptions to the NO OVERHEAD FIXTURES rule. Drum shade pendant lamps do make a style statement in modern spaces, particularly if hung in multiples, but don't rely on them to throw the majority of light into the room. (This is fashion before function, honey.)

Consider hanging four grouped in the center of the room if it's large enough; a smaller room can handle a pair.

Drumshade pendant lights are super-chic in multiples.

Arrange drumshade pendants geometrically in large rooms.

Don't skimp on the size of drum shades; they should be at least 15 inches in diameter and can be as big as 22 inches. To avoid your guests looking like they're wearing funny party hats, though, forego the drum shade treatment unless your ceilings are at least 9 feet high. Be bold when choosing shade colors—it's a perfect moment for statement-making colors like taupe, black, whatever bouncy accent color you've chosen for your room, or even patterned fabrics.

Lightbulbs

Vary the wattage of lightbulbs in the room to create drama and direct the eye. Brighter bulbs belong around the sofa area so that you can see the people you're talking to; dimmer bulbs are lovely in more discreet areas, where you don't really need to see what's going on.

New lamps are always labeled with the maximum wattage bulb that can be used in them. Take this number seriously, doll (says your tester who's already burned out more than one lovely lamp by persistently ignoring the recommendation). As a general guide, install a three-way (50-70-150 watt) bulb next to your sofa, 40- to 60-watt bulbs in lamps set on a credenza, and 60- to 75-watt bulbs in floor lamps meant for reading. Sconces that really must illuminate a space should get 75-watt bulbs rather than the 40- to 60-watt bulbs used for decorative lighting (so take the max wattage into consideration before you whip out your Amex for new ones).

DESIGN DETAILS

Lampshades

Lampshades in a living room don't need to all match but should have a pleasant dialogue among themselves re: style, size, shape, or color.

TRADE SECRET
When shopping for new shades, always take the lamp with you to the store and try them on there before buying. And, sugar, there are *no* exceptions to this rule. ✱

Books

Books look great in any room in the house, but especially in the living room. That said, don't confuse the living room for a library. Think of your books as accessories, not outfits. Lay them out according to the size of the room; line a stretch of wall with them (you can put a wide sofa in front of them). Otherwise pair them symmetrically throughout the room, use them to delineate zones (that's for you apartment dwellers), or position them to flank the sofa. If you opt for the latter, station smaller end tables in front of them to hold lamps.

Taller bookcases are great for adding height to otherwise architecturally void spaces. Lower bookcases seem to work better on the shorter walls in the room; when they are pushed up against long walls, they chop up the expanse.

Built-in bookcases are terrific, but expensive. Choose them only if you own your home or are married to a carpenter. If you rent and can't live without built-ins, make sure they are constructed so that they can be taken apart and taken with you when you leave.

Needless to say, freestanding bookcases are the more mobile option. Don't let those budget-busting built-ins intimidate you, doll, especially when even the *cheapest* bookcase looks great once it's filled. Selecting the cleanest lines and most minimalist frames for budget freestanding bookcases helps make sure that what's in it gets more attention than the bookcase itself. And I'm still a fan of the clean-lined simplicity of adjustable shelves on wall-mounted metal standards for the renter.

Disguise mass-produced bookcases by decoupaging paper on them. Newspaper classifieds, gift wrap, craft paper, wallpaper—they all make clever covers for a run-of-the-mill set of shelves. Affix the paper with glue diluted with water and, once it's dry, apply two or three coats of polyurethane on it with a wallpaper squeegee.

Note to you paperback hoarders (including my husband): Paperbacks. Are. Cheesy. (Although the larger "trade" paperbacks aren't too shabby.) Banish them to the basement (although Goodwill could sure probably use a donation or two!) and show off your hardcovers in the living room instead.

Art, Photos, and Objects

Art over the sofa should be in proportion to the size of the sofa, i.e., *big*. *Create* big when necessary by grouping lots of smaller pictures together. Add 3 inches all around to the perimeter of your art when matting, or a minimum of 2½ inches, so that the art "pops" visually in the frame. For groupings with more than one row, the spaces between images should be the same vertically as horizontally. As a rule, this shouldn't be more than 1½ to 2 inches. These images should be identically framed, since you're using them to make up a single unit.

For a more modern touch: Hang art asymmetrically over the sofa. Vary the sizes and frames, but be sure to fill at least 50 to 60 percent of the 5-foot-high space above the sofa with art. Unify your modern grouping by using the same-colored mat for all the images. Experiment with your layout on the floor before hanging; start with the images in an elongated horizontal diamond shape (stretch out one "side" of the

TRADE SECRET

Allocating an inch to an inch and a half of space between frames is usually fine. Very large images (on lots of wall space) can often take two inches, but rare is the grouping that requires more than that. When you're aligning rows of frames, use the same spacing between rows vertically as between frames horizontally. To jazz up rectangular groupings, try indenting every other row. *

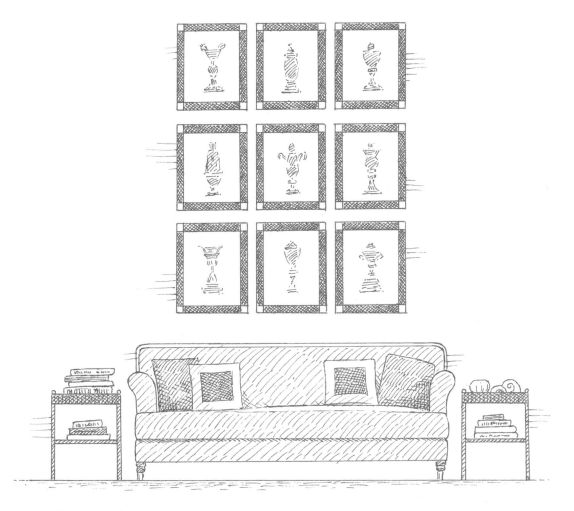

Art over the sofa should fill at least two-thirds of the available space.

diamond farther than the other), and move them around from there.

Decorative or antique plates look great above sofas in traditional rooms, but don't skimp on quantity for the prettiest look. (Quality, on the other hand, is irrelevant. I love shop-

Arrange multiples of art in larger geometric shapes, like a rectangle.

ping for antique plates on eBay!) Lay your plates out on the floor first to find an arrangement you like before hanging them on the wall. Try different geometric shapes for your grouping—diamonds, squares, rectangles, circles, or even X's work well. Use plate holders to hang them; find these in a hardware or home goods store's picture-hanging supplies department.

Group collections such as your forty thousand family photos stylishly and powerfully in one place (as opposed to scattered all over your house, which gives much less of a visual impact). Bookshelves and étagères (open-sided, freestanding bookcases) are perfect for this. Use one color of frame to unify the bunch, like silver or black. (The frames themselves shouldn't be identical.) Use the étagère to display the collection only; mixing other stuff dilutes the effect. This rule works for displaying almost everything you collect: Anything over 6 inches tall goes on shelves; under 6 inches may be better seen on a table top—use your visual judgment.

Throw Pillows

Throw pillows should never all match. Typically we group a pair of 18-inch square pillows with a pair of 16-inch square ones. At the most, the same-size pairs can match (but they don't *have* to). It's also pretty to add a small rectangular fifth pillow, between 10 by 12 inches and 12 by 14 inches, in a totally different fabric. (This is called a *kidney pillow*; place it closer to one side or the other, and not floating all by its lonesome in the center of the sofa.)

Use a touch of a citrus or a sherbet color to add splash. Throw pillows with orange, coral, or, especially, yellow in them fit the bill beautifully and, I promise you, will work in almost *any* room. Remember that solid vs. pattern rule, above.

All-down fill is loveliest for throw pillows, but 100 percent feather fill or even all Dacron will work just as well if you're

Five throw pillows on an 84-inch sofa look fabulous.

on a budget. The secret is to make sure your pillows are over-stuffed (but not exploding).

Final Touches

If you're floating a sofa in the center of a small room and don't have enough space to put a console behind it, don't leave the back barren: Drape a textile that's close to the width of the sofa over the top of the back (leave 6 to 8 inches clear on each side for the sofa to peek out from beneath), and let it hang down to just above the floor (or just above where the sofa legs start). Lay the textile flat on the sofa and let it hang straight down—this trick doesn't look right when the fabric is draped or pleated. Exotic printed throws, pretty patterned quilts, and antique textiles work marvelously.

Other living room rules to live by:

- A touch of Asian style looks great in almost every room and chicly varies the style-scape. It can be a tiny tea table, a lacquered or carved tray, or a Ming-vase lamp. Narrow Chinese consoles are always great wherever you're lacking depth.
- And don't forget the power of a dash of black—whether in a picture frame, a tiny table, or an accessory, the most basic color instantly ups the style ante in any room you put it in.

DINING ROOMS

2

They're about so much more than food. Formal dining rooms are meant to be dramatic backdrops designed to enhance your home's star of the show: *you!* Everything else (like what you're serving for dinner) should come in a distant second. The secret is, you spend so little time in your dining room that it's the one space in your house that's safe to make almost as theatrical as you dare (see Laundry Rooms, Chapter 9, for tips on unleashing your ultimate design fantasies, unfettered and in their wildest state); you'll rarely get tired of the scheme. So when you're dreaming up your dining room's décor, it's safe to err on the bold side and knock it out of the park, stylewise. Make it memorable for your family, your guests, and, most of all, for *you.*

THE LAYOUT

For my fellow city dwellers thinking, *"dining room, yeah RIGHT"* right about now, know that the first rule about dining rooms is that you don't need a dedicated room to have a sophisticated place for your friends and family to share a first-rate meal. Here's the scoop, dahling: If you are formal-dining-roomless, carve out space for a dining area somewhere else, like in your living room, den, or foyer. Dining tables can look great stationed at one end of the living room or den; round tables can be fabulous in a foyer (although you may want to limit foyer dining to special occasions rather than nightly dining, with rental chairs that politely *leave* when the party's over and don't require storage).

Another winner if you're really short on space is the dining room/library/office combination. In this setup, bookcases look great along as many walls as your room's size allows—at the very least, lined at least along one wall or maybe strategically placed in the corners of a smaller-size room (the units should be identical and wide enough to not look like scrawny grasshoppers on stilts brooding in giant, empty corners), with your dining table floating toward the middle of the room. Transform your credenza or filing cabinets into perfect sideboards for the evening by tossing a runner or table-cloth over them. Work your table lamps so the room oozes ambiance and remember to relocate those piles of files you've

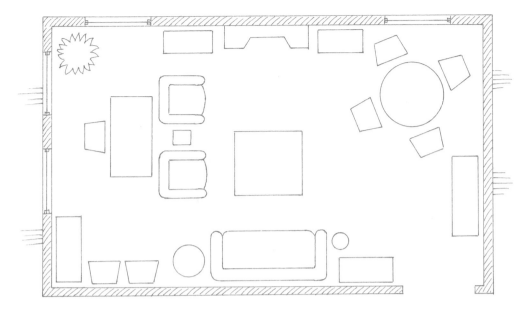

Create a dining zone at one end of your living room.

been meaning to get to forever to the closet or under the bed for the night. *Dinner is served!*

Delineate the dining zone in a multipurpose room with its own area rug. However, leave the space rugless for contrast if there's already a large rug anchoring the room's main seating area. Think *long and hard* about putting two competing rugs in one room; if you've just gotta do the two-rug two-step, though, let the larger rug be the star (i.e., patterned) and opt for something streamlined, textured, and fairly patternless, like sisal, simple pile, or berber, for junior.

Dining Room Basics

For you lucky devils with real dining rooms (i.e., not New Yorkers), here are a few rules to follow. Distribute your dining room furniture in a balanced fashion throughout the room, not lopsidedly. Excess symmetry can be ho-hum in other rooms, but it's a dining room's best friend, so let it rule your layout. (Symmetrical setups are calming to the eye, which means you'll admire the view once and then focus on the tasty treats in front of you.) Always start at the center of a wall. However, if there's a niche at one end of the room or in a corner, station something in it, too. In gigantic dining rooms, adding at least one tallish piece of furniture like a highboy on the center of one wall (or symmetrically, centered on opposing walls, if you scored a pair) helps vary the scale. Station extra chairs in pairs along an empty wall or flanking sidewall furniture to visually fill the space. Always aim to keep your layout balanced, so the room doesn't seem to tilt excessively in any direction when you stand in the center of it: Have a little action going on every wall, even if it's only art (see below).

Walls parallel to each other should feel similarly "weighted." Employing oodles of art to visually fill an empty wall that's directly across from a furniture-laden, or window- or arch-filled wall is one of decorators' oldest tricks in the book.

Nothing says "dining room luxury" like richly paneled walls and elegant wood trim. If you opt for wainscoting (that's the waist-high paneling seen in formal rooms and stair halls), its top should be about 36 to 48 inches above the finished floor. Chair rails, once designed to actually protect delicate painted and plaster finishes from abusive bumps by wayward chair backs, should top out at 34 to 36 inches above the floor.

If you do go for an area rug, make sure it covers the floor at three key points: when the chair is stationed under the table, when it's pulled out for a person to sit down or get up, and when a person is seated in it comfortably. (While we're at

Add a tall piece of furniture, like a highboy, to vary the scale in your dining room.

it, dahling, know that rugs go a long way toward absorbing the cacophony of noisy dining rooms—a plus!—but lord, can they be crumby! [a minus], not to mention annoying to slide your chair across when sitting down. So pick your battle wisely.)

SIZE MATTERS

The most important size to get right in your dining room is, of course, the size of your dining table. Here's the rule: The size of your dining table should relate to the size of your dining room . . . *and* the size of the groups that you need to have seated for dinner. Some good-to-know numbers:

- Dining tables should be 30 inches high. Allowing 18 inches of table width per person is a good rule of thumb, but feel free to squeeze that number to 6 for holiday dinners (just kidding!).
- A few other measures to live by:

Square and Rectangular Tables
A 30 × 36-inch square seats 1 to 2 people
A 30 × 38-inch square table seats 4 people
A 40 × 48-inch square table seats 6 people
A 40 × 72-inch rectangle table seats 8 people
A 48 × 96-inch rectangle table seats 12 people

Round or Oval Tables
A 45-inch round diameter seats 4 people
A 66 × 45-inch oval seats 6 people
A 73 × 45-inch oval seats 6 to 8 people

The Great Table Shape Debate

Your table's shape should relate to the overall shape of the dining area's space: A rectangular room calls for a rectangular or oval table, and the closer the space your table occupies is to a square, the better a square or round dining table looks in it.

Knowing how much space you *really* need to maneuver around your dining table can be a tricky proposition. Allow a minimum of 44 inches from the edge of the table to the wall. Make it at least 54 inches if you have a sideboard, chest, or server stationed on the wall—leaving 3 feet of space between the table's edge and the front of the sideboard will give you room to pull out your chairs and navigate seating comfortably. Overfilling your room with so much furniture that it's hard to walk comfortably around the table is a no-no—if you have a tiny dining room and a classic Italian family of twenty-eight for holidays, then, baby, set up a buffet in the dining room and a larger table in the living room for the night! And keep your daily seating for six neatly in place for the other 364 days a year. For you Californians with the opposite problem (we're jealous again!), a wee little bridge table in your 3,200-square-foot dining room is the equivalent of too thin and too rich.

Getting the chair height right is also important. Unless you want your guests to feel like Little Miss Muffet on her night out at a hookah lounge, opt for seating that's at least 16 to 18 inches high from the floor to the top of the seat. If your chairs have loose seat cushions, count their heights in the 16- to 18-inch number, so folks still have room to cross their legs under the table.

Sideboards

Now that you know all there is to know about dining room tables, let's move on to the next-to-the-biggest piece of furniture in the room, the sideboard. There are only two rules to adhere to when choosing a sideboard: It should be the second-largest piece of furniture in the room after the dining table (i.e., not borrowed from a doll house, doll), and the two should *never* match. Take size and style into consideration based on the amount of space you have.

If your dining room is small, your sideboard will likely need to be both smallish and shallow, as well. If you can't find an appropriately sized piece you like, a pair of matching pieces (two small chests, Asian consoles, etc.) will do the trick. Butt them up right next to each other (no space in between) to give the illusion that they're a single unit. Drape a runner long enough to span both pieces over the top to keep up the ruse.

Whatever sideboard you chose, it should look good morning, noon, and night (i.e., even when it's not showcasing your inner Julia Child). Station a pair of lamps, a piece of sculpture, decorative plates on stands on top—anything that can be easily removed when the surface is called into active duty.

NOTE: Now, china cabinets aren't sideboards, but I'll have a little word with you about them here, anyway. I know *noooooo* dining room in my native South is ever complete without at least one china cabinet in it, but your Decorator Girlfriend here just can't wrap her head around them, for some reason. I loathe them! But out of deference to the land of my birth, ladies, if your grandmother would just roll over in her grave if her china was displayed in anything other than a mahogany china cabinet, please make sure that the one you choose is appropriately sized for your dining room—an overly large one can instantly shrink the room by a third.

THE COVER-UP: STYLE AND EFFECT

Walls

In a small space like a dining room, wall treatments can make a big statement. Nowhere else can wallpaper be more stunning than in your dining room, so I encourage its use with *abandon*—the wilder, the better. (Even if your own personal idea of wild and crazy decorating doesn't go far beyond stripes!) The larger your room is, the bigger and more outrageous your wallpaper pattern can be. If you're not a pattern kind of person, a fabulous texture, like grass cloth or Madagascar cloth (that's a more raffia-looking type of woven grass cloth), can add visual warmth to your walls without being a distraction.

For the truly adventurous, stenciling your grass cloth or even burlap wallpaper (that's burlap fabric that's been backed with paper by the manufacturer so it can be applied as wallpaper) with an oversize motif (damask? geometric? gorgeous?) using several complementary paint colors is a guaranteed recipe for incontournable chic.

If you'd rather stick with paint (and honey, that's *okay*), let the time of day you most use your dining room dictate its color and mood:

- If you use it primarily at night, and it's not a room you pass through frequently, opt for rich, deep-hued drama (think red, brown, persimmon, navy, teal, avocado, etc.).
- If your dining room's high-volume moments take place mostly at noon (are you legendary for your Sunday power brunches?), but it still isn't a high-traffic pass-through, then go a little lighter than the deep, rich hues without excessively dialing down the drama—opt for tobacco instead of brown, dark French blue instead of the deepest teal.
- If you pass through your dining room nonstop (i.e., en route to the refrigerator), avoid the deep, dark colors and rein in the richness for a more peaceful passage with khaki, buttery yellows, pastels, pale gray, taupe, or ecru. Bring in the decorative

high drama through lavishly patterned and/or hued chair upholstery, curtains, tablecloths, napkins, and area rug.

Furniture Style

When furnishing your dining room, think about how dinners will flow *chez vous.* You'll need something to eat on, *natch,* something to lay out food on buffet-style, something to sit on, and something to see by. Those are the basics—everything else is decorative. Looking for the perfect dining room furniture? First thing to know: Matchy-matchy dining sets are passé. Now, if you're first learning of this major development in the design field *here,* honey, I am *sorry* to be the bearer of bad news! But my Southern and New England ladies, despair not! If you've inherited marvelous pieces from your grandmother and great aunts, then you get a pass on this trend. When buying new furniture, though, absolutely, positively *refrain* from purchasing a matching set! The chairs should all match each other (unless you station a pair of contrasting ones at the ends of the table, from which you and your regent may reign while dining) and *complement but not match* the table. The chairs and the table should complement but not match the sideboard. Ask yourself, "Do these look good together?" and you'll never go wrong. Feel free to combine painted with stained woods and mix together different periods and styles. Asian sideboards, cabinets, and chests look great with traditional chairs and a contemporary table.

To encourage guests to sit and linger, it's hard to beat upholstered dining chairs for comfort. At minimum, choose an upholstered seat; for maximum cushiness, upholstered seats *and* backs. Never lean back on your dining chairs' rear legs (your mother was right!)—they weren't built to stand that and I promise you one day . . .

LIGHT THE WAY

After great actors, one of the most important parts of any theatrical production is lighting, and your dining room is no exception. Go the extra mile to get the lighting just right in the room, and you'll reap the benefits night after night.

Divide your dining room into lighting zones, each with a separate task—lighting what's on the table, lighting who's at the table, and lighting what's in the room. And whatever you do, make the light indirect rather than direct. *So* much more flattering! In a perfect world, each should be on a separate electrical switch—so each can operate independently—and put on dimmers, too.

Chandeliers

There are chandeliers and there are Chandeliers, the drippy crystal numbers that look just smashing in a Vegas showgirl's dressing room. Avoid them not only because they'll make *your* room look that way, too, but also because you sit too close to them in most dining rooms to, er, appreciate them. Under duress, they may work in a foyer or entranceway, but that's not where we are right now, darling. So pay attention! Here are my chandelier basics:

- The key to getting the chandelier right is to match its style to the style of your dining room, or choose the opposite route and hang one that contrasts *dramatically.* A super-traditional chandelier looks fab in a modern space and, likewise, a minimalist one gives an edge to a traditional interior.

- Other than by diameter (*obvious!*), chandeliers are defined by their lines (curlicued, straight, etc.), material or finish, and the number of arms that they have. As a rule, straighter lines say modern while very rococo, curvy baroque-esque chandeliers, such as those made with Murano glass, are more traditional. They always look fantastic because they read as both lighting and sculpture. Classically inspired, clean-lined shapes look great in any space.

- If your chandelier is painted, it should complement the rest of the room's décor. Metal chandeliers should either match or complement the color of the door hardware in the room; if your hardware is brass, choose a brass-based antique finish. If the room sparkles with satin nickel hardware, make sure some is shining in your chandelier, too. And just like your fashionista friends keep telling you, black (as in wrought iron, black metal, and black paint) goes with *everything*, sugar, so when in doubt . . .

- If one arm of your chandelier burns out, don't despair; have it rewired. Should one of your chandelier parts be damaged (the faux candle arms, etc.), replacement parts are available online using the search words "replacement lamp parts."

Chandeliers light both what's on the table and also your lovely guests. They should be proportionate to the room they're in *and* the table that they're over. Here are two formulas design pros use to help them calculate chandelier size (but at the end of the day, trust your own judgment—or that of your most stylish friend!—and know that it's better to err on the smaller size and not vice versa):

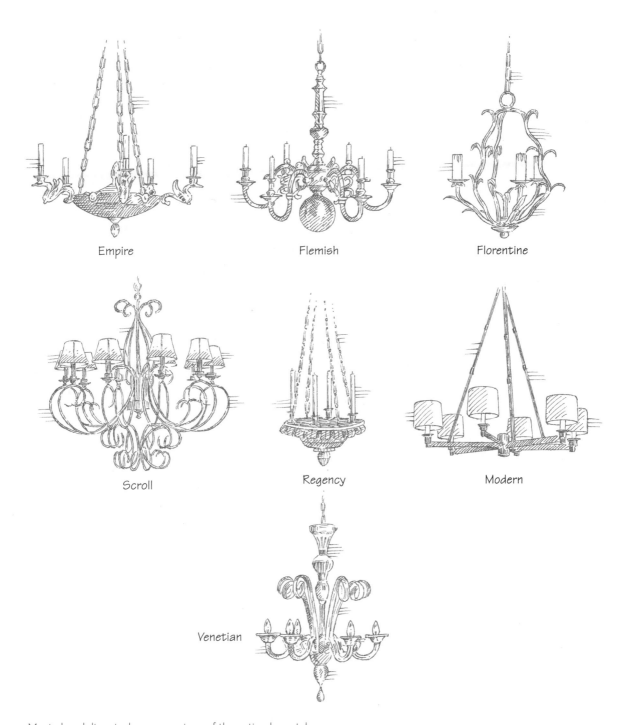

Empire

Flemish

Florentine

Scroll

Regency

Modern

Venetian

Most chandeliers today are versions of these timeless styles.

- Divide the width of your dining table by two to get an approximate chandelier diameter (so for a 48-inch-wide table, start with a 22- to 24-inch-diameter light).
- Add the room's length and width in feet; the sum equals an approximate chandelier diameter in inches (so for a 10 by 12 room, 10 + 12 = 22-inch diameter to start with).

Once you have the correctly sized chandelier, hang it 30 to 36 inches above the table surface. Let both common sense and your ceiling height be your guides, here, sugar—if you have an 8-foot ceiling, a too-low chandelier dangling in front of someone's forehead when they're sitting will *definitely* distract from the conversation!

Now that you've gotten the chandelier business together, the rest is easy! Wall sconces are great options for illuminating your dining room's walls. In smaller dining rooms, installing a pair of sconces on each of the longest parallel walls will do the trick. In more palatial settings, consider a pair or more on each wall of the room. Center your sconces' back plates between 60 and 64 inches above the floor, depending on your ceiling height.

Design Tip

If you have a very large dining room table, adding recessed lights at the ceiling, in addition to the chandelier, can provide general lighting for the dining zone and also help your crystal to glisten and gleam.

I also love table lamps on sideboards for eye-level lighting. Narrow candlestick lamps with smallish shades don't take up

Hang your chandelier far enough above your dining table to not bump into it when you stand.

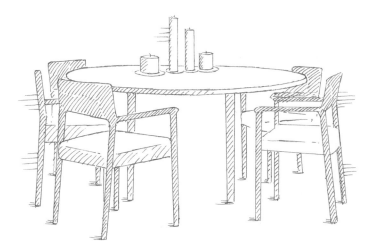

loads of space and deliver a complexion-flattering glow. *Love* them, love them, love them! But if you turn on your little candlestick lamps, try not to turn on the wall sconces at the same time—that tends to be too much of a good thing, lightingwise!

DESIGN DETAILS

You can have *sooooooooooo* much fun with accents in a dining room! First of all, don't neglect your dining room walls. In sparsely furnished rooms (which the dining room by

Candlestick lamps on a sideboard + wall sconces = chic.

definition technically is), what happens on the walls becomes of tantamount decorative importance. Maximize your visual impact with mirrors—the more the merrier. I'm crazy about filling a wall with a grouping of small-size bargain mirrors (think 12 inches wide or less). Stack them in multiple rows of odd numbers (like five rows across over five rows down), without too much space in between each mirror (spread the grouping out on the floor first to check your layout, but as a rule, know that between 1½ and 2 inches is best; anything over 2½ inches is almost always too much). It's a setup that's simply *magical* by candlelight.

Oversize pieces of art look great in dining rooms on otherwise empty walls, too. Think big—like 48 inches wide and up. Remember, though, that the larger the canvas, the farther away from the wall you have to stand to visually appreciate it, so if you have a tiny little dining room . . .

Shower the open space under consoles, sideboards, or serving tables with attention. For traditional dining rooms, large-scaled decorative objects like antique urns work visual wonders; in modern spaces, try a piece of sculpture, an organic element like a grouping of driftwood logs, supersize decorative boxes, or clean-lined Asian trunks.

Most important, if you're still saving up to buy the dining room furniture of your dreams, don't deprive yourself of the pleasure of using the room in the meantime! Pick up a set of inexpensive folding chairs (and a set of cheap and cheery

Don't leave the space beneath a console empty.

cushions to put on them since, honey, folding chairs weren't *designed* for *comfort*) at a garage sale (done!) and an appropriately sized folding table (ditto!). Dress it all up with stunning tablecloths from your favorite discounter, light masses of candles every night, and dine in style and splendor until you can upgrade. *So* chic! Bon appétit, my lovelies!

BEDROOMS

3

It's the first place you lay your eyes on in the morning and the last thing you see at night—your bedroom is
the room that you should love best of all. There's no
more personal a space in your entire home, which
means you're *morally obligated* to make it nothing less than your
very own sybaritic paradise, outfitted to be as comfortable
and relaxing as humanly possible. We spend one-third of our
lives sleeping; that's *a lot* of time to spend in one room, even
if you used it for nothing less! (And *who* just uses their bedroom for sleeping? Show me a bedroom that doesn't multitask!) You want it to be dreamy to fall asleep in, divine to

wake up to, and pure pleasure in the light of day. If you have small children, it's even *more* important to splurge on the master bedroom: It's far less likely to be at risk for destruction than the other public rooms and, sugar, *every* parent deserves a safe haven.

Every bedroom, whether lilliputian or larger than life, requires the same basic elements: somewhere to sleep, someplace to put your things while you're sleeping, lighting, storage for your clothes, and a resting spot for clothes on the way into or out of the closet. And (space-starved friends ignore this one): someplace to sit and contemplate how great life is (although we still want you to contemplate the greatness of life at every occasion! You'll just be doing it on your bed, not next to it). If you're a throw pillow aficionado (i.e., you live south of the Mason-Dixon line), you'll also need someplace to put your collection of eight fluffy pillows in starched embroidered cases while you sleep. Very little of the above should match—*nooooooo* matchy-matchy ever—with the exception of the nightstands and lamps. If you have lots of closest space, store all of your clothes in it and use any other furniture in the room for more exotic purposes. Fill that chest of drawers with your lingerie, accessories, or out-of-season clothes. *Luxurious!*

THE LAYOUT

If your lair is exceptionally spacious, divide it into zones: one each to sleep, sit, dress, and store. If it's less-generously proportioned, you can still do all of those things; it's just a matter of scale. No matter the size, though, remember that more of the floor in the bedroom is covered with furniture than any other room in the house, and on top of that, windows and doors eat up wall space, too. What this means is that it's important to think your layout through . . . and through . . . to get the most out of this most personal of spaces.

Here are four space-maximizing bedroom layouts:

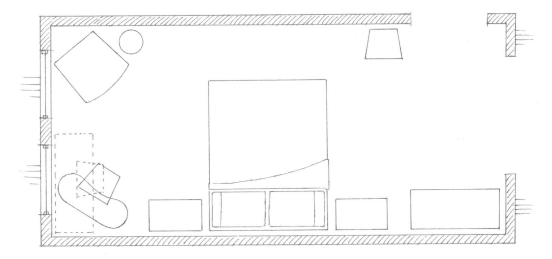

The long, narrow bedroom.

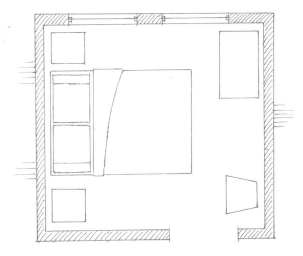

The square and boxy bedroom.

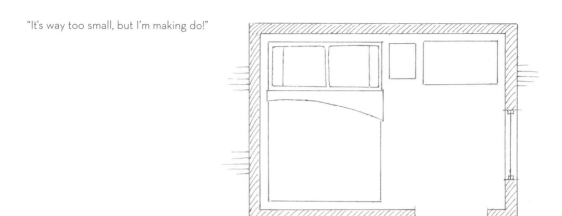

"It's way too small, but I'm making do!"

The palatial bedroom.

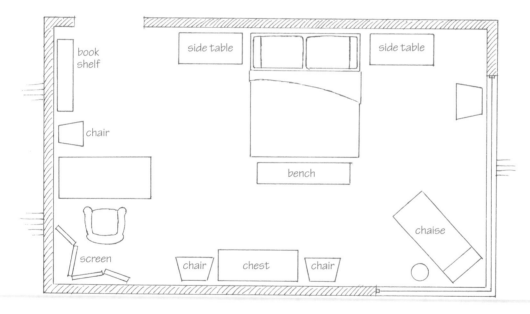

BEDROOM BASICS

The biggest question when it comes to the bedroom is where to put the bed. As a rule, the head of the bed should run along the room's longest wall. But don't hesitate to change its location in a small or awkwardly shaped room in order to maximize space. If the "true center" of the wall is off (i.e., it sits in a niche and the "sides" of the niche aren't the same size), try positioning the bed at the *faux* center first—that is, in the center of the niche and not the true center of the wall. And then choose whichever position pleases your discerning eye. Wherever you position your bed, try to leave at least 24 to 36 inches clear all around it, or on two sides if you've pushed the bed's long side up against the wall, so that you can walk around it easily.

If you're burdened with an overabundance of windows (honey, we should all have your problems!) and are running

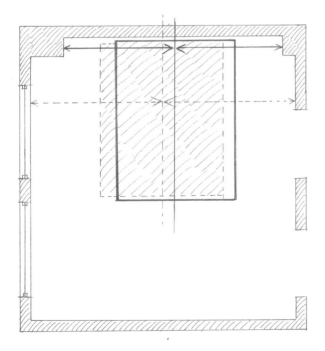

Station a bed in the center of the niche, not the wall.

low on wall space, don't be afraid to "sacrifice" a window if your bed truly looks best positioned in front of it. (Helpful hint: The window will be on what seems to be the room's longest "wall.") Keep the window treatment minimal, like an outside-mounted roman shade (more on window treatments in Chapter 10) and hang loads of art on the walls on either side of the window. Keep the art and bedside details fairly symmetrical with this setup because you're trying to achieve balance, and every bit helps. If you are more of a maximalist, install floor-to-ceiling curtains at the window behind the bed, extending the curtain width to about 3 to 4 inches past your headboard on either side. Hanging sheers behind the curtain panels helps camouflage where the real window ends and the wall begins makes the window look larger and transforms the curtains into a superstar focal point for your now-stunning bedroom.

Rule of Thumb

Angling a bed out into the room is a cute editorial trick that is impractical in real life, unless you live in the Taj Mahal. It looks off-kilter! And, darling, don't let anyone tell you differently.

If you have sufficient space, benches, chests, boxes, or trunks at the foot of the bed are as functional as they are chic. Make them proportionate to the size of your bed; use multiples to create length if necessary. Stylewise, your options are endless—upholstered or wooden benches, Asian trunks, vintage suitcases, oversize English mahogany cellars, sleek modern

Camouflage that window behind floor-length sheers and daringly station your bed in front of it.

lacquered/leather/wooden boxes, upholstered cubes—anything that is just slightly lower than the height of the bed and no more than 15 to 21 inches deep. They're perfect nocturnal destinations for the 42,000 pillows that decorate your bed during the day, not to mention the three outfits that you wore last week but haven't gotten around to hanging up yet, and/or this week's/month's/year's reading material.

An armchair is a definite bedroom must if you have the room. They look fantastic angled in emptyish corners. So what if you'll never actually sit there? A lovelier clothes rack you'll never find! If there's space for an ottoman, too, that's awesome, but skip it if space is tight. In smaller bedrooms, choose a dining-size chair instead of an upholstered arm-chair. Station a floor lamp behind the chair, and position a tiny table to the side, ostensibly to hold a book and/or drink (*as if*). In minuscule bedrooms, an armless chair, a bench, or a cube (upholstered or not) can get the job done. If there isn't room in a corner for your chair, other great locations for "the drop" include wall space between doors or windows.

The wall space between two doors (i.e., the bathroom and closet) is also great for a dresser or a desk if there's at least 36 inches in front of it. You want to be able to pull out those drawers comfortably.

Congratulations! Your Bedroom Is Huge

If you're one of those lucky devils fortunate to have a cavernous bedroom, then *make the most* of that space! After squaring away your bed + nightstands zone, turn your adoration to the room's remaining walls. If you have the space, nothing beats a seating area in front of a window. (Be sure you have ample room to walk around it, doll.) The parallel loveseat/settee/chair layout, to be avoided like the plague in your living room, actually works marvelously in your bedroom, primarily because the chances of actually sitting there and talking to someone are slim to none! Bedroom seating tends to be for eye candy only. (Not that we want to discourage you from using it—*au contraire*!) Other options: a desk against or perpendicular to a wall, a chaise longue angled out into the room, and of course all of the above if you live in the Taj. See the illustration on page 52.

In a supersize bedroom another fabulous space-eating ploy is a writing desk area. Float it in front of a window so it becomes a "room" unto itself that will never intrude on your resting hours. Your printer and/or fax can go adjacent to the desk, on a tiny table (one with a shelf is a plus) not much larger than the unit itself, whatever size that may be. If you live in the states of California, Texas, or New Jersey, you will undoubtedly have room to have a *pair* of these cuties flanking your little desk; use the other table to attractively stack books, magazines, office supplies (display them on one large tray on the tabletop, all in attractive containers stolen from your kitchen, bath, or local gift shop), or those framed family photos that keep breeding like rabbits (all in similarly colored frames). Vanity tables with adorable little chairs do the trick beautifully, too—all the better to see you with, my pretty!

Nothing fills seemingly endless corner space in a bedroom—in any room, actually—better than a gorgeous folding screen (note we said gorgeous), whether deliciously antique, custom upholstered for your space, or a marvelous flea market or discount find. It adds a nice textural layer to the room and also just looks fabulous in general. Set a chaise in front of it, angled out into the room or parallel to your screen. Don't forget the floor lamp and tiny side table, the latter no higher than 18 inches or the arm height of the chair/chaise, and no more than 12 to 18 inches in diameter or a same size square.

If you have a vast bedroom, chances are that you also have an equally vast closet to match, so don't feel obligated to put a dresser or chest in your room, just because. On the other hand, if you happen to come across one of the giant, oversize mahogany mamajammas that are sliced thin and stacked high, with drawers and cubbyholes galore, why resist? You've got room! And they're fabulous. Perfect for gym socks, because you'll probably already have cute little bins for everything else in your walk-in.

Your Bedroom Is Cute and Cozy

When laying out small bedrooms, it's okay to bend a few rules for space. Go ahead and put the bed perpendicular to the wall so that the long side of the bed is against it. True, making the bed will be sheer torture, but you'll have maxed out your space, which is worth it!

It's not necessary to keep a small bedroom empty, but you do want the furniture that you put in it to be on the skinnier side of the scale. Opt for a full-size bed instead of a queen (see below), with diminutive bedside tables. If you don't have room for bedside tables, station your dresser next to your bed and set your lamp on top of it—but don't use it as a night-stand (it's too tall). Set a teeny-tiny table (9 by 12 by 18 or so) between your dresser and the bed to hold your nighttime essentials.

A bench or desk or dining chair along a wall can visually fill an awkward bit of empty space (use the chair or bench as a clothes drop). But if you're among the impressively neat who won't be using the chair as a hanger (sigh), set up a pretty still life of objects/plants (orchids were *created* for the purpose!) and/or books and magazines, etc. on it. Lean a framed print on top against the wall (the art should be smaller than or the same size as the chair). Definitely hang a piece or two of art or a mirror on the wall above the bench—you're creating an exciting visual destination that adds another layer of stylistic depth to your bedroom.

For very small bedrooms, station your dresser in the closet if you're gifted with more closet space than wall space.

SIZE MATTERS

Honey, the size of your bedroom furniture is crucial! It's your sanctuary—you don't want to overstuff a small room or underfurnish a palace. So here we go:

Beds

It's the *bed*room, so getting the size of your bed right matters most. Goldilocks wants you to know that the standard sizes of mattresses and box springs from smallest to largest are: twin, twin extra-long, full/double, queen, queen extra-long, king, and California king. And the dimensions are:

Twin	39" × 66 to 76"
Twin Extra-Long	39" × 75 to 80"
Full/Double	54" × 75 to 84"

Queen	60" × 80"
Queen Extra-Long	60" × 84"
King	76" × 80"
California King	78" × 84"

You definitely want to test-drive a new bed before you take it home. Shop around and by all means, flop right down on it in the showroom—for a good ten minutes, doll, don't rush—until you find one that feels just right. As a guideline, your bed should be no less than 6 inches longer than the tallest person sleeping in it. And at the very least, make sure it's wide enough for all parties to link hands behind their heads without any elbows *or pets* hanging off the edge.

Beds should be proportionate to the room that they're in. As we discussed above, if your bedroom is minuscule (a promising trend in new construction today), I promise you will be happier with a full-size bed rather than a queen. A mere 6 inches wider than a full, a queen's additional half foot of space makes as much a difference in your personal roll-over room as it does in visually overstuffing the space. The full's smaller scale does wonders to keep the room from looking crowded, so be a style trooper and resign yourself to one, sugar. If you have a 600-square-foot bedroom (i.e., 20 by 30 feet—did I mention California, Texas, or New Jersey? But I speak as a jealous New Yorker), you're going to need a king-size bed. Other furnishings—nightstands, desk, chaise, dressing table, folding screen, etc.—should be fairly generously sized, too, and in proportion to the bed. In a tiny bedroom, pair your full-size bed with mini-size everything else.

Today's trend toward supersizing and overstuffing means that within each category, mattress sizes and thicknesses can vary from manufacturer to manufacturer. So be sure to verify the measurements before signing on the dotted line, and that goes for buying bedding, too.

Headboards

Upholstered headboards are one of the easiest ways to add a little oomph to your bedroom on the cheap. Almost every catalog and online merchant offers one at every price point known to man. You can never go wrong with the straight-lined variety—it's the little black dress of headboards. Depending on the fabric that adorns it and the pieces surrounding it, your bed can be fit for Audrey Hepburn or Madonna. Regency-shaped headboards with curvier tops are more traditional; tufted styles can go either way. The sparer the tufting, the cleaner, more modern the look.

Here's the scoop on obtaining a perfect headboard height: Headboard height should be directly related to the height of your assembled mattress, boxspring, and bed frame, *plus* the height of your pillow setup on top of that. If you'd like anything taller than that, the rest is gravy.

Pillow size cheat sheet:

- Standard: 20" wide × 26" long
- Queen: 20" wide × 30" long
- King: 20" wide × 36" long
- Square Euro Sham: 26" × 26" square

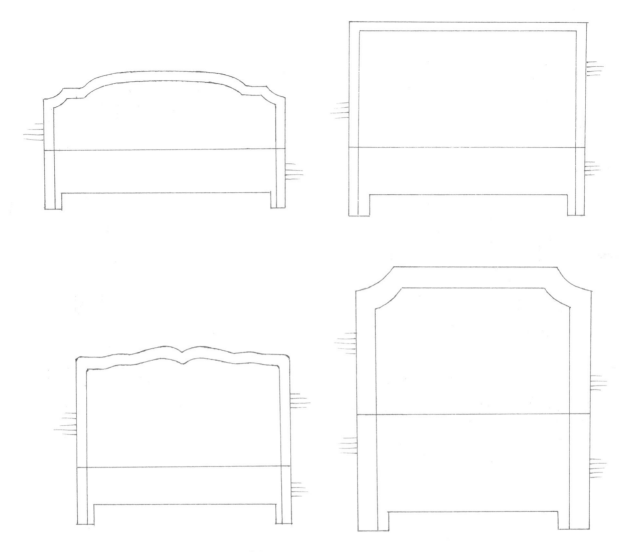

Upholstered headboards go with every style of décor.

Have a look at these heights, to get your creative juices going:

- 47" tall for headboards that don't show a lot of headboard above the pillows

Tufted headboards take on the style of the room around them.

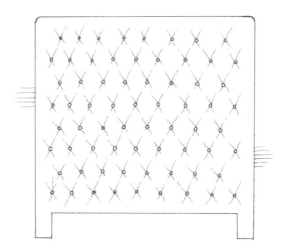

- 52" and up for headboards that show more of the headboard above the pillows
- 54" and up for headboards that show LOTS of the headboard above the pillows

Rule of Thumb

Remember that if you like to dangle your feet over the edge of the bed while you sleep, you are a prime candidate for a bed with a headboard only and no footboard.

Bedside Tables

Bedside tables should never tower over your bed once you're supine. They look best either at or just below the height of your dressed bed. The dressed part is important here—if you're an ascetic, your bedding will add a mere inch or two, but if you're going for the duvet-upon-double-blankets Princess and the Pea look, your bed can grow by almost a foot! That said, for most beds, 24 to 27 inches is a perfect height for a nightstand. King-size beds require proportionately sized nightstands (that means wider, doll), or the pairing will look like Jack Spratt and his wife plopped along your bedroom wall.

In terms of width, choose bedside tables large enough to accommodate a lamp, telephone, books, and water glass at the very least. If wall-mounted swing-arm lamps are part of the setup, it's okay to forego the space for lamps.

For a king-size bed, anything smaller than 28 inches wide starts to look a little like Twiggy next to the Fat Lady—36 inches and up works *so* much better proportionately, sugar.

Another note: Bedside tables don't have to match but should not be wildly disparate in height. A couple of inches difference is okay; half a foot will look lopsided. A desk is a terrific option for one side of the bed as a bedside table, if you have room. Go for a smaller desk—24 by 48 is a brilliant size, and narrower secretaries with drop-down desks are perfection—because you want the desk to be smaller than the bed (which a humongous partner's desk is not). In small bedrooms, go beyond the bed stand for creatively chic night tables that won't hog what little space you have. *Tabourets* (that's French for "small table"), upholstered or solid cubes, tiny tray-top tables, and wall-mounted shelves and brackets all are stunning, simple, and, most important, *slight* alternatives.

THE COVER-UP: STYLE AND EFFECT

Furniture Style

News flash: The days of the five-piece matching bedroom suite are over! Extreme matchy-matchy is a no-no in any room. Even though your five-piece might be attractive in the right setting (KFC?), it's always better to go for a mix of pieces that visually complement rather than mimic each other. Paired nightstands are okay; everything else should simply look lovely together—think similar lines, shapes, or colors, with the occasional odd piece for oomph . . . exactly the way you'd furnish your living room! *(NOW you're decorating like the pros!)*

One way to add great drama to a bedroom is to have a four-poster bed, but keep your ceiling height in mind. Nothing looks better in a room with ceilings 9 feet high or more, but do *not* go there if they clock in at anything less, or you'll end up emphasizing the very element (low ceilings) that you're trying to downplay. (If you're blessed with Texas-size ceiling heights, the converse is true: avoid low-slung or platform beds like the plague, or your room will look like Snow White's palace in the Land of the Seven Dwarves.)

A word about art and the four-poster: Hanging large art behind a four-poster bed interrupts the regal lines of the bed and looks crowded. Hang either a single small item there—like a 12- to 14-inch starburst mirror or one little painting—or a dainty, smallish-size grouping of demurely dimensioned images.

Basic, Beautiful Accents

If you don't go for the four-poster, it is virtually impossible to overfill the space above your bed, no matter what type of headboard you choose. Don't neglect it—it's one of the few spaces that you can decorate to your heart's content. Fill it with lots of different-size images, in complementing but not matching frames, arranged either symmetrically (more

TRADE SECRET
All of the rules that cover mixing different furniture styles in your living room also work all over your house, so cross-reference them when making selections for your bedroom, too. ✱

Keep art behind a four-poster bed light and lean.

traditional) or asymmetrically (not traditional); a series of same-size, identically framed pieces, laid out in a square or rectangle; or a single, large image that takes up at least two-thirds of the space above the bed. Think out of the box to avoid that hotel-art feeling.

Hang wall accents over your bedside tables as well. Paired pier mirrors—they're long and narrow—look great over bed stands. Have a custom set inexpensively made to your specifications by your local budget framer. Depending on your ceiling height and bedside table width, mirrors hung vertically, sized 25 inches wide by 59 inches tall, could be just what the doctor ordered for elegance. (Make them 2 to 3 inches narrower than your bedside table's width, and about

There's no such thing as overdecorating the space above your bed.

two-thirds of the available clear wall space above the bedside table for height.)

In styling your bed, one handy trick of the trade is to fake an upholstered headboard by propping a pair of rectangular shams in a contrasting color against the wall. Then lay two sets of pillows *flat* on the bed in front of them—don't prop them up like the shams, or you'll lose the headboard effect. Choose a heavier fabric with lots of body for your shams so they don't wilt and stay plumped, propped, and plushly vertical.

A bedskirt can look sloppy unless it is custom-made for your bed. However, precious few are the folks with custom-made bedskirts, so here's how to get a custom-looking fit from a store-bought skirt: Remove your mattress, arm yourself with T-pins or safety pins (T-pins are easier to work with; get the biggest ones) from a fabric or craft store, and neatly pin together the bedskirt's excess fabric in a vertical "seam" from the foot of the bed to the head. Plop the mattress back on top of your box spring, and nobody will notice your handiwork but you! Alternatively, an upholstered box spring on decorative legs (why not have it match your headboard, too) eliminates the need for a bedskirt.

Courageously mix and match your bed linens, blankets, and shams. But make sure the top and bottom sheets match each other and that the pillowcases do, too. You want the bedclothes to complement each other, but they don't have to be identical.

Rule of Thumb

If your college graduation was more than seven (seven, and we're being generous) years ago, then it is a design felony for you to be sleeping anywhere near a futon and/or sleeping loft on a permanent basis (although overnight visits are of course permissible). Period.

Chests of Drawers

- The path to choosing the right dresser for your bedroom is short: Pick one based on the amount of space left over after the bed is in the room. City dwellers who are short on space should avoid the temptation of jamming a plus-size dresser into a pint-size bedroom (we understand that you truly *do* need the space, but not nearly as much as you need to walk around your room without bumping into the furniture). To this dilemma I say, *get creative, dear.* Rethink your closet space, and while you're looking at the possibilities in there, purge yourself of everything you haven't worn in three years.

- In a wee-size bedroom, dressers can serve as nightstands. This is the one time it's okay to break the bed table height rule. Station a teeny, tiny table in front of the dresser, pushed a bit closer to your bed, for stashing your night-time essentials (honey, only Lurch would able to reach them on the dresser while lying down). Put the bedside lamp on the dresser and attach an on-off switch to the cord (they're sold at the hardware store, or a lamp repairman can do one for you) so that you barely have to move a mus-cle to turn it on and off.

Bedroom Floors

Whether it's bare, wall-to-wall carpeted, or a delightful hy-brid of both, your bedroom floor should pass your bare feet's "smooth and warm" test (so no marble or other tile). This is a room where the flooring doesn't have to stand up to intense traffic, so feel free to indulge in both ends of the quality spectrum in that department—either the insanely luxurious or utterly cheap and cheery, both of which tend toward the delicate (although for different reasons).

Wall-to-wall carpet is better-suited for bedrooms than any other room in the house. It's virtually unbeatable if you're a fan of sinking your toes *deeeeeeep* into softness first thing in the morning.

For the coziness of wall-to-wall *and* a little bare floor airi-ness, too, opt for an oversize area rug that covers most of your bedroom floor. Make sure it's large enough to comfortably sit your bed and nightstands; it should extend 6 to 12 inches beyond the outer edges of the nightstands and the end of the bed.

Rule of Thumb

While we're at it, here's a great rule of thumb for bare floor exposure with area rugs: In small rooms, leave 4 to 7 inches of floor clear around the rug's perimeter; 12 to 15 inches clear in larger rooms; and for medium-size rooms, somewhere in between.

Much-smaller rugs on the non-bed floor space can also look good—5 by 7, 4 by 6, or smaller-size area rugs do the trick perfectly, depending on the available clear floor space on either side of your bed. Whatever size, it's okay to sit an area rug on top of your wall-to-wall for added texture, color, and style, especially bedside where your feet hit the ground running in the morning. There should be contrast in the weaves of the carpet and the rug—if one is dense and thick, the other should be significantly thinner.

Should all four of your bedside tables' legs rest on the area rug? As a rule, the taller the legs of your bedside tables, the better they will look resting on the rug. Taller tables or leggy units with upper drawers just look more stable this way. It's okay to float the tables 3 inches or so out from the wall to accommodate this (which looks way better than the alternative, pushing your rug all the way against the wall on one side!). On the other hand, chests of drawers and other short-legged pieces look fine with the front legs on, rear legs off. Whatever the case, the front exterior leg should always be ON the rug!

LIGHT THE WAY

Proper lighting is as important to an inviting bedroom as high-thread-count sheets. To get it right, think not only gentle and romantic but also task. Without well-placed lighting, your romantic Zen bedtime moments will most assuredly be frequently interrupted by eyestrain.

Swing arm lamps rule in bedrooms. Not only do they liberate your bedside tables from one extra object, but they can also be adjusted to cast light at the most advantageous angle for your reading pleasure. Mount them no farther than 3 inches out from the edge of your headboard (or, if you are headboardless, the edge of the bed) and high enough so that the bottom of the shade is about 20 inches above the top of your mattress. If you can, try actually sitting in bed before mounting your sconces to find out precisely the best location for your height. Floor lamps are another great option for the tiny bedroom, especially just next to the bed when the lamp providing overall bedroom lighting is more than two feet away (i.e., out of arm's reach to say good night).

BTW: *Why* people put tiny little lamps on their bedside tables is *beyond me*! Standard-size (22 to 27 inches tall, with shade) table lamps look so much better! As a rule, the bottom of the shade should be about 20 inches above the top of the mattress. If you have a cute, girly dressing table, save your boudoir lamps for that. Short on bedside table depth? Re-place round lampshades with shallow oval-shaped ones.

For a lamp on a dressing table, here are some measures worth knowing: The bottom of the lamps' shades should be about 15 inches above the surface of the table, assuming you're sitting down to primp! If the top of your dresser serves as a waist-height dressing table, the bottom of the lamps' shades should rise 22 inches from the top of the dresser. And remember to always make up by paired lights.

Swing arm lamps direct light to where it's needed for reading.

DESIGN DETAILS

As in the rest of your palace, the rules of yin and yang hold true for your bedroom. Opt for a balanced combination of shiny and matte, nubby and smooth, patterned and plain. An all-shiny bedroom will look like Greta Garbo's boudoir, an all-over patterned space will ultimately give you a headache, and an overdose on austerity will remind you of Cellblock D. Here are some more tips for great details in your lair:

- Fold a throw in half (if it's small) or thirds (if it's larger) lengthwise and lay it flat across the foot of your bed. Actually, the foot of your bed looks better with *anything* folded neatly across its length (including your partner). Think duvet covers (empty or full works equally well), extravagantly textured blankets, perfectly patterned window panels, even fabric shower curtains (fold them so you can't see the grommets or loops). The extra texture not only adds warmth to the room; it also stylishly hides the unsightly "seam" where the box spring meets the mattress. But be sure the textile/throw/whatchamahoo extends the full width of the bed and, preferably, drapes down a little on each side, or it'll look like a postage stamp stuck in the center of the envelope of your bed, which is *so* not cute.
- Drape a sheet, a throw, or a length of fabric lengthwise across the top of your four-poster bed for added visual appeal. You can gently "pleat" it (okay, *bunch it up*) for a lush effect or lay it flat for a tailored look. The ends should hang over the sides by 12 to 18 inches.
- Ban boring storage from your bedroom! Add a row of built-ins along the wall beneath your windows for extra

TRADE SECRET
Did you know that you can shop the kitchen cabinetry departments of big box stores for amazing bedroom storage cupboards? Their talented in-house planners will help you lay it all out. If you are bereft of nightstand drawers, stylishly display creams, potions, and nocturnal unguents in pretty trays, on plates, and in boxes that complement the room's personality. Track down these bedside beauties in the bath, kitchen, and office supply departments—lacquer tank top trays and boxes stack beautifully and look fabulous, for example, so you can have a perfect night's rest knowing your bedside tables are stunningly styled. ✷

storage. Top them with 3-inch-thick cushions (either made-to-measure, or simply pile on discount store throw pillows with exuberance) to create inviting window seats.

- Do I *need* to remind you to use coasters on your nice night-stands? Make them the cutest coasters in the house, too, honey. You look at them twice daily, every day!

POWDER ROOMS 4

After the kitchen, the powder room is probably the most-often-used space in your house. It's definitely the one that guests see the most . . . and are likeliest to shamelessly investigate in excruciating detail once they close the door! So aim for yours to pass the Powder Room Secret Police inspection with flying colors. (With these nifty tips, that'll be a piece of cake.) Not in the least of reasons why is because most powder rooms are minuscule. In fact, a *palatial* powder room is an oxymoron—unless, of course, you live in Texas. These tiny spaces should unequivocally be about more, more, more, no matter what your style preference is. Think of them as the christening gowns of your home—the more elaborate the design, the better. Spare no detail (and no expense either, *especially* if you're on a budget). Whether guests have the privilege of seeing the rest of your house or not, you want any visitor who needs to wash his hands to marvel at your great style and/or taste while doing so. If no one exits your powder room talking about how amazing/creative/unusual/beautiful/provocative/_____ (fill in your accolade of choice) it is, then, honey, it's not done up enough! Banish the banal; take it to the limit, and then push the envelope some more. If you're thinking of gold-leafing your powder room, for example, be sure not to miss a square inch! Why? Because you can—in this small a space, going hog wild with finishes and fixtures that ordinarily cost millions per square foot will only set you back $129.99!

THE LAYOUT

The powder room is technically a "water closet" (or "W.C.," the term architects and designers use to designate bathrooms; "water closet" in its purest sense is what your toilet is called, since toilets were originally located in closetlike spaces), consisting, as a rule, of a sink and a toilet. (And a bidet, if you are a fancy pants Francie.) Laying this room out is rarely rocket science (unless you're trying to find space to squeeze one into an existing home, which can admittedly be tough.)

If you're building a powder room from scratch, as silly as it may sound, remember that sound carries—consider where your powder room is . . . and what's audible to folks on the other side of the door. In terms of size, try to make it at least 7 feet 9 inches by 3 feet 4 inches if the toilet and the vanity face each other in a shoebox-size space. Here's the math: Toilets range in depth from about 27 to 32 inches, which means you need a space of about 4 feet 6 inches from the back of the tank to the wall to accommodate your knees while seated. Add 1½ feet to stand in while you wash your hands at the sink, plus the average vanity depth, 21 inches. For the width of the tank, allow 30 to 36 inches of wall width; the minimum width of ready-made vanities is 18 inches (24 inches is the next size up, which is much more comfortable). Some experts insist that the center of the sink should be at least 18 inches from an adjacent wall, but designers know better—that can't always be the case.

The Skinny on Sinks

Let your square footage determine your sink style. Sink/vanity combos are the chicest things ever, if you can fit one in your powder room, and nothing makes a cuter vanity than a gorgeous chest, dresser, or commode that fits your style. Be *vain* about your vanity! The piece should be 33½ to 38 inches tall, countertop included. Have your carpenter cut the back out to accommodate plumbing pipes (drawers, if any, will no longer function, so seal them shut with wood glue; tape the drawers shut with blue painter's tape until the glue dries), and add a marble or other surface top if you like. If you prefer, you can drop in, undermount, or surface-mount a sink basin directly to the chest or table's top surface, but seal it with polyurethane first to protect it from water splashes and drips. Asian chests and tables come in lots of colors and all sorts of small sizes, and go with every single style of décor if you're crunched for space.

Another option for smaller powder rooms is to have your stonemason whip up a stone or marble top and apron that mount directly to the wall. (They look like they're floating, but are invisibly supported by a wood and/or metal frame below.)

Great shapes for stone or marble wall-mounted vanities.

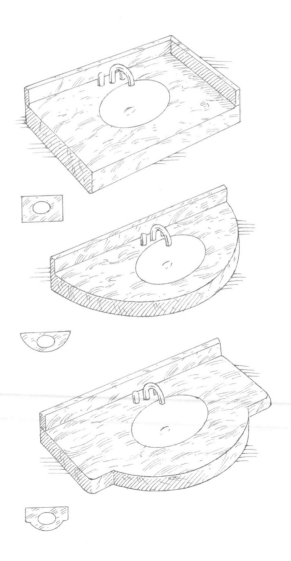

Keep in mind:

- Freestanding pedestal sinks are also great for powder rooms, particularly if you aren't one to fancy a piece of furniture in your loo.
- Wall-mounted sinks are just what the doctor ordered in the tiniest of spaces. Resort to a wall-mounted corner sink under extreme duress, only, though; darling, I'm afraid they're *coyote ugly*.
- See Bathrooms (page 137) for other exciting sink tips.

SIZE AND SHAPE MATTERS

In these small quarters, proportion makes a big difference. Think of your mirror and your vanity or pedestal sink as a *pair*. You want them scaled appropriately to each other. Subtract 6 inches from the width of your vanity if it's more than 24 inches wide (for widths less than that, subtract 4 inches), and now you have your perfect mirror width. For the height, the mirror should be tall enough to fill at least 66 to 75 percent of the wall space between the top of the vanity and the bottom of the light. If you have a surface mounted bowl-type sink, the mirror should end far enough before the top of the bowl's edge to avoid splashes.

Since you're not *reeeeally* going to be using your powder room to primp every morning, opt for style over substance and choose a regular wall-hung mirror rather than a traditional recessed medicine chest. It's much more sophisticated. Choose a frame that matches your style at the local framer's, or snag an antique model that's relatively close to the perfect size

The mirror should be proportionate to the vanity beneath it.

for your setup at the flea market. If you find an antique mirror with a stunning patinated frame, have your framer replace the cloudy glass with new mirror; the better to see you with, my pretty.

If you go the custom frame route, know that you can combine frames of a similar depth into one mackdaddy mirror frame for absolute chic. Round mirrors also look great in powder rooms, but they should be more than 18 inches wide so they don't look like portholes on the *Titanic*.

THE COVER-UP: STYLE AND EFFECT

In even the most subtle, subdued, Zen-master domains, powder rooms should be dramatic, detailed, and daring. Whether you opt for discreetly luxurious materials—think limestone, Venetian plaster, milk glass, and platinum (yes, *platinum*) fixtures—or a more visual cornucopia of do-it-yourself decorative delights, make sure something exciting is happening on the floor, on the walls, *and* on the ceiling (good taste traditionally dictates that only one of these may outshine the others in any one space, with the rest relegated to supporting cast, but, sugar, powder rooms never follow the rules!). I once papered a powder room with a plate-motif fabric and then hung real antique plates on the wall over the loo, which would have been *de trop* in any other room of the house. Make "more is more; busier is better" your decorative mantra for these jewel box spaces.

Creating Stunning Walls

Let's start with those statement-making walls. Painted walls will do as a starter, but don't stop there. Choose dramatic paint colors like red, black, orange, olive, brown, fuchsia, taxi-cab yellow, or whatever bold hue tickles your fancy. Tape off 9-inch segments and stripe your walls in elegant tonal stripes: Select the darker color first, and then go two tones lighter on the paint swatch for your contrast hue. (When actually painting, however, the lighter color goes on the wall first as a base.) If your powder room is truly tiny, 7-inch-wide stripes may work better, but as a rule, anything narrower than 9 inches starts to look circusy, as, by the way, do stripes of dramatically contrasting colors like red and orange (although they are adorable in children's bathrooms).

Whatever you put on your walls next, sugar, put *lots* of it. Mementos from trips, family photos, architectural relics, your grandmother's plate collection, your collection of vintage dog leashes, Christmas ornaments pinned to the wall, newspaper clippings from important events in your life, your children's school pictures, report cards—all of this is fair game for plastering on your powder room walls, from floor to ceiling. Yes, you should frame them. No, the frames don't have to be identical. (But they should be complementary.)

Wallpaper also looks divine in powder rooms, especially richly patterned or textured styles that are too outrageous for larger spaces. Center large patterns on the wall, especially if the walls are not wide enough to accommodate the entire pattern. Faux woven leathers, bolder grass cloth weaves, and anything else that's too delicate for larger rooms is a great choice for the powder room. If you are a patient and creative genius, make your own wallpaper from newspaper, graph paper, or gift wrap—affix to the wall with thin white school glue diluted with water to resemble a soupy paste. Run a wallpaper smoother over each pasting to smooth it out and eliminate air bubbles, as you would regular wallpaper. Staple a gorgeous swath of fabric, pulled taut on every wall, affixing it just below the ceiling and above the baseboard, then hot glue decorative ribbon or trim over the staples to hide them.

A classic look for a powder room is gold-leafed (or any other metal leaf) walls. If you're maxing out the metallics, have your ceiling contrast the glistening walls in a complementary color, like a silver or bronze ceiling paired with gold walls. Alternatively, choose a dramatic paint color for the ceiling and stencil geometric pattern—I love a Greek key—along its border, in either leaf or a contrasting color. Check out floor tile border patterns for ceiling border inspiration. If your powder room is under the staircase or tucked into any other spot with a low, sloping ceiling, however, treating the ceiling the same as the walls helps blend the two seamlessly together.

Another dress-your-wall idea: A chair rail (which is basically a piece of molding running waist-high along a room's perimeter) installed at 36 to 38 inches above the floor is terrific in a powder room, and it lets you double the fun on your walls! Contrast your finishes/papers/fabrics above and below your chair rail.

The Best Floors in the House

Great powder rooms start at the ground up; that is to say, with your fabulous floor. The smaller the room, the grander your floor should be—it's eye candy for the sole! Even if you're channeling Monastery Chic in ten thousand shades of white, your powder room floor should be dazzling in both material and detail. Material should be as opulent as your budget can stand; detail should take into consideration your floor's border, field, and center, plus its baseboard trim, with something exquisite happening at every level. Marble tiles are the cat's meow for powder room floors. Now, I am the *champion* of ceramic tiles for every other room in the house (honey, they do a *good job* with those fakes these days!), but I'm encouraging you to go for the Real McCoy for your powder room, primarily because you'll only need about six tiles to complete the whole job! Choose tiles that are dramatically veined, in either the most fanciful colors or in the deepest ebony black. Pair your floor with a marble baseboard, between 4 to 7 inches tall, depending on your ceiling height. (BTW, 3 inches is the absolute minimum height for a marble baseboard; anything less looks stilted and is visually underwhelming.)

Since the powder room is tubless and therefore not in a high-risk flood zone, wood flooring also looks stunning in them. Continue whatever hardwood floor runs throughout the rest of your house, or choose one that dynamically contrasts the floor adjacent to it (and, by the way, this is the only time you get to do this with your wood floor in your whole house; the rest of the floors should all be virtually identical, so knock yourself out). Don't forget the drama: Lay your floor out in a herringbone, basket weave, or *even fancier* pattern. Don't forget the contrast inset border around the perimeter of the room. Opt for the most exotic woods you can pronounce (or have to learn to!); the border should be detailed, too.

Another idea is to rim a parquet floor with a border of mosaic stone. Pair your fancy parquet pattern as a field with a breathtaking—and sold preassembled on mesh, so it won't become a Big Craft Project for you—mosaic stone border around the perimeter. The stone should directly touch the wall, with a wood baseboard on top of it. Adjust the width of the border to the size of your room: In a 4-foot-wide room, for example, a 6- to 6½-inch-wide stone border looks great. Run a single row of complementary contrasting tile (like black) around extreme edges of the tile, inside and outside, to really set it off. NOW you've got a floor that'll get them

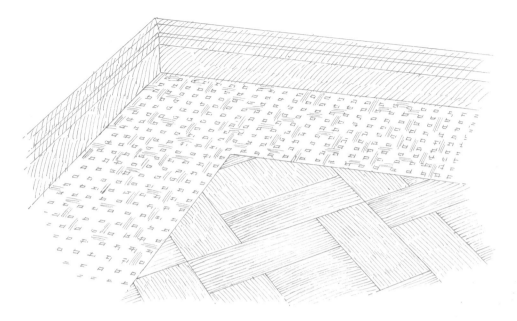

Pair a wood parquet field with a mosaic tile border for drama.

talking! Which is the whole point of decorating your powder
room to begin with, dahling.

If your budget puts the kibosh on luxurious materials, then
up your powder room floor's style ante by dramatically laying
out simpler goods. Go for the boldly laid-out oak parquet
floor, or stain straight-run planks in fabulous three- to four-
toned trompe l'oeil, rug-inspired patterns (don't worry—the
floor is small enough for you to be finished by the time all
that stenciling starts to drive you insane). Style-up ceramic
tile by laying it in the most dramatic patterns, too, fantasti-
cally bordered or not; consider pairing the faux-tile field
with a mosaic border of real stone or marble (be sure to
match the tile thickness or compensate on the floor for the
difference). Cabochon insets (the little contrast diamond

Cabochons add budget drama to ordinary tile floors.

squares that are geometrically scattered throughout larger tiles) add depth to ho-hum fields.

Leather tiles are the pinnacle of chic for any powder room floor. I'm crazy about them on walls, too—either on one wall (i.e., behind the toilet wall in a long, narrow space) or below the chair rail all around. With a dramatic border, of course. Yes, they're millions of dollars a square inch (I exaggerate!), but for a *tiiiiiiny* little powder room . . . And you'll love how they wear like lovely old shoes. For these most fabulous of floors, install a wood baseboard that matches the baseboard throughout the rest of the house, finished to complement the powder room walls (and not the floor). If water hits them, give them the same TLC you'd give good shoes that got caught in the rain. Buff them regularly, and you'll have a lifetime of luxe that makes you smile every time you walk into the room.

LIGHT THE WAY

Powder rooms are all about vanity. They're where your guests—and you, after serving that third round of drinks—will be glamming it up. That said, they should have also perfected their makeup before leaving home! So although it's not about studio-quality hair and makeup lighting—we're talking *strictly touch-ups* here!—getting the lighting in your powder-your-nose right is of paramount importance. Here are the essentials:

- Light from two sources is a must: a ceiling light to illuminate the room, and something closer to the mirror to illuminate your reflection. Locate the primary ceiling fixture in the center of the room. Then consider a discreet recessed spin spotlight above the center of the mirror, at least 18 inches out from the wall, to light that space. In a perfect world, you should be able to look up and see the light *just in front of you* when you're standing at the mirror. If it's directly over your head, it will cast a shadow and you'll be standing in pitch darkness in your reflection. It's worth the time and effort to get the position of this light right. Side- or above-the-mirror wall-mounted sconces work well, too. (Having a wall-mounted fixture + an over-the-mirror, ceiling recessed fixture = amazing light, BTW.)

- Don't limit your powder room light shopping to the bath department. *Au contraire!* Choose wall sconces, chandeliers, and pendant lanterns from the general lighting department—anything that would look great in your living room, foyer, or stair hall is exactly what you want for the powder. Wall sconces also look great in a narrow room above the loo. Just don't get carried away with the Sconce Moments, though, or your powder room will start to look like a college library (and your overdue books will distract you from applying your lipstick).

- Put each light on a separate switch so they may be operated independently, all on dimmers for ambiance, of course.

- Play with the lightbulb wattage for each of your fixtures until you get a level of lighting that works for you. Remember, we're going for soft, glowing ambiance (that borders on *dim* until you raise the dimmers once you've closed the door).

- Chandeliers are great if your ceilings are at least 8 feet 6 inches. And even then, opt for a *smaller-size* number, not Venetian Palace Jumbo. Under 8½ feet, choose a pendant lantern hung close to the ceiling (no more than 3 inches of chain, really) or a groovy surface-mounted fixture.

- The simplicity of recessed lighting can't be beat in low-ceilinged powder rooms. Install four high hats, each about a foot or so in from a corner; or in a truly tiny space, use two equidistant from each other and the four walls. ONLY install a single light in the center of the ceiling under penalty of death; they cast the most unflattering shadows known to mankind and I wouldn't wish that on you for the *world.*

- If your powder room is under a stair, with the dramatically sloping ceiling that accompanies this setup, then definitely consider a wall-mounted sconce (or two) as lighting. Install one on the longest wall, toward either the center or the rear of the space; the other can go on the narrow rear wall above the loo. Also consider a single recessed ceiling spotlight above the mirror and no sconces flanking the mirror (too much of a good thing, sugar). Think about what would most evenly illuminate your space when you're laying it all out.

DESIGN DETAILS

Here are a few more design essentials and tips for a gorgeous room to powder your nose (*and* impress your guests):

- After you spend all that time (and we won't mention *money*) whipping up the most fantabulous walls in the universe, *avoid* ruining the effect with a *towel bar.* Not only do towel bars take up valuable wall space (where you should be hanging lots of art!), but in this germophobic era, five thousand people sharing a single guest towel is, um, gross (even if it *is* heirloom Irish linen). Ditto bar soap. Luxurious paper towels are *so* much more elegant for the modern style maven! Stack them on a stunning rectangular towel tray to the side of the sink, and splurge on nice *liquid* soap, too.

- Leave your powder room floors bare; all the better to see that spectacular floor.

- Again, it's perfectly fine to display family photos in your powder room if you're a casual-style household (or if they were taken by Irving Penn). *Especially* if you display *lots* of them. Mount them floor-to-ceiling in similarly colored frames or pick one style of a clean-lined frame in varying colors.

- Amass mounds of potted orchids on your toilet tank, either real (if your powder room gets sunlight) or faux (if it doesn't), in cute cachepots.

- And, finally, don't forget a stylish wastepaper basket (which you should empty frequently; honey, we all tend to forget), scented room spray (leave it on the countertop, next to the liquid soap), and (luxurious, great-smelling) hand lotion, too. *Now* you're ready for company!

KITCHENS

5

Whether you're in there whipping up gourmet meals for twelve or merely replating your takeout du jour, kitchens are the soul of every home. Like bathroom design, a lot of what actually makes a kitchen functional and easy to use is formulaic. So in a room in which so much is ruled by standard layouts, heights, and widths, it's paying attention to teensy details that'll give you the most opportunities to express your own style. A wall cabinet is a wall cabinet is a wall cabinet, but its door style, hardware, and interior are all about you. *Imagine:* If every granite countertop on your block were identical, what you displayed atop yours would still make it unique. Bereft of lovely objects, cute containers, and fabulous art, dahling, most kitchens would actually resemble high school science labs (*especially* since stainless is all the rage)! Warm, elegant kitchens are all about great accessories and style minutiae that say *you*! Which means that you're officially free and clear—and *strongly encouraged!*—to *accessorize away* in yours.

THE LAYOUT

Choosing an appropriate kitchen layout is as important as picking the right life partner. Actually, a quality kitchen can outlast many marriages these days, so like your mother said . . . Choose carefully and find one that that really works for you 150 percent.

Design Tip

Save yourself a gray hair or two, and let a big box store become your bestest friend *the very minute* your first "new kitchen" thoughts *occur*. Sugar, they've figured it *all* out, eliminated all of the guesswork, and will make the whole new-kitchen process *a breeze*. All you have to do is accurately measure your space (let me repeat, *acc-u-rate-ly*), take your dimensions to the store, and let their super-talented kitchen planners handle the rest. They'll work with you to develop the perfect customized layout, help you select door styles, finishes, and countertops that reflect your taste, *and* hook you up with a highly qualified person to install it all. Comparison shop until you find a planner you adore. If you're not on a budget (*sigh*), you can also work with a kitchen specialist (they do all kitchens, all the time) or a private contractor. The beauty of these tradesmen is that *they* come to you. Check the National Kitchen & Bath Association's Web site, www.NKBA.org, for more info on working with a kitchen specialist and tons of other tips, too.

When considering your layout, the first thing to know is that the *work triangle*, or the layout of your stove, refrigerator, and sink, is the kitchen's golden fleece, the pivot around which everything else revolves. Here's the scoop: *When you draw an imaginary line from the stove to the refrigerator to the sink, it should form a triangle and* not a square. You will tread this path endlessly while demonstrating your culinary genius. Depending on your kitchen's size, the triangle's three sides should add up to between 12 and 23 feet (although if you live in New York City, it's fine if yours just adds up to 3).

Now that you know the importance of the work triangle, here are six basic kitchen layouts, each named for the way its counters are shaped:

• A *strip* kitchen features one single countertop with everything on it (and no work triangle). As a rule, a strip kitchen should be no more than 22 feet in length, with the sink centered along the strip (unless you plan on making cooking a prime exercise moment of your day).

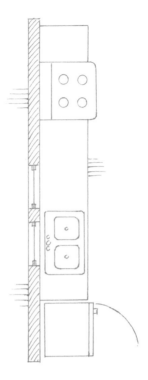

The strip kitchen.

- A *galley* or *corridor* kitchen has two countertops running parallel to each other, with the appliances and countertop work space divided between them. Setting up your work triangle in a galley kitchen is a snap; locating the sink and stove (*stove = range = oven*, BTW) on the same counter helps minimize interruptions and increases work space on the other side.

- An *L-shaped* kitchen is just that; it runs along two adjacent walls with the refrigerator at one end, the range at the other, and the sink in the middle. The long leg of the "L" can also serve as a room divider in spaces that combine the kitchen with an adjacent dining area.

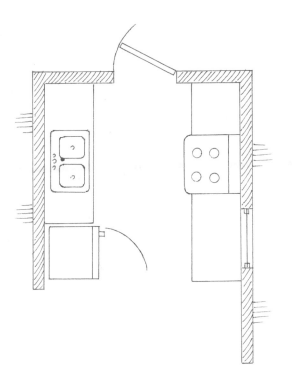

The galley kitchen.

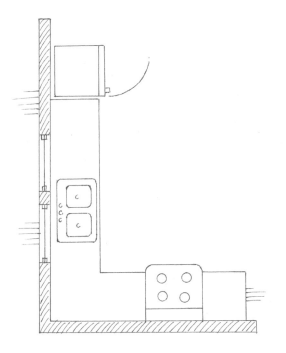

The L-shaped kitchen.

The U-shaped kitchen.

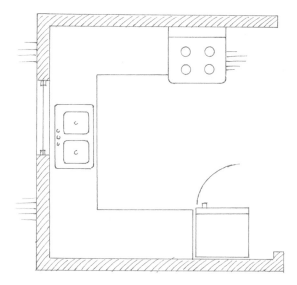

- A *U-shaped* kitchen is the tailor-made solution if you can use the words *large* and *spacious* to describe your kitchen (and *jealous* to describe the rest of us). Each leg of the U incorporates one element of the work triangle. Typically the sink goes at the base of the U, with the oven and refrigerator on the facing arms. City dwellers, be warned, though: if there's less than 6 open feet between the base cabinets, you're in for a *tiiiiiiight* squeeze (unless you are named Twiggy).

- A *G-shaped* kitchen adds a peninsula to one end of the U-shaped kitchen. (Ta-da!) If you're the kind of cook who needs your solitude, this may be the layout for you; claustrophobics, on the other hand, can feel hemmed in by that extra jog in the countertop.

- An *island kitchen* expands work and storage surfaces and divides a kitchen into functional work areas, via a freestanding "island" floating in its center. The island can be mobile or fixed, which allows you to install a cooktop or a sink in it and gives you a spot for eating, too. Make your kitchen

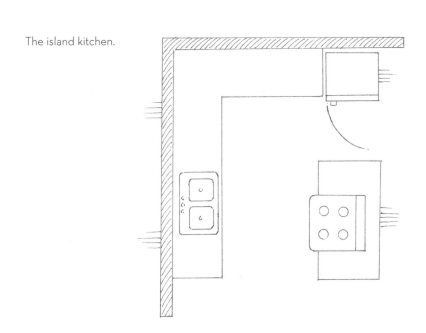

The G-shaped kitchen.

The island kitchen.

island from your base cabinets and countertop surface: Mount two rows of cabinets back-to-back, or one set with a countertop that overhangs the cabinets at least 9 to 12 inches for dining. (A typical dinner plate is 9 inches round, so 12 inches is best if you can.) If your island will be Hangout Central, a 15-inch overhang will encourage your peeps to do that. Include a center support beneath the overhang if you have heavy countertops, and always allow 3 to 4 feet of floor space clear all around for navigation. Install electrical outlets on the island's sides to juice your appliances (discreetly start with the side farthest from the kitchen's door, so the plugs will be less visible).

For you foodies, gourmets, and gourmands who read cookbooks in bed and can zest a kumquat blindfolded: Cherubs, y'all are *above and beyond* the run-of-the-mill, basic work triangle. Make it a starting point, instead, for your dream kitchen, which will undoubtedly feature built-in oven(s), indoor grills, his-and-her dishwashers, and oodles of other fun bells and whistles that don't need to fall within the W.T. since they aren't used every day. (Although if they *are,* then honey, we should all be coming to *your* house for dinner tonight!) Do try to keep your workhorse of a microwave within the W.T.; put it near your fridge, where what gets cooked in it comes from. At the end of the day, aim for efficiency and walking the fewest steps, Chef Tell.

Here are other important tips for a fabulous, functional kitchen layout:

• If you can, avoid putting your dishwasher in a corner or on the same side as the work area or stove. That'll allow you to open its door while cooking, brilliant multitasker that you are, and will also free up the work area's cabinets for stashing pots and pans.

- No oven is an island unto itself: Free-floating ranges are a no-no. Make sure there's at least a foot of work surface on either side of the range or cooktop to serve as a landing strip for dishes entering and exiting the oven. Sitting the range next to a tall cupboard, wall oven, or refrigerator is another don't—if you can't spread your arms from side to side while standing at the stove, you'll feel like the kitchen is closing in on you when the burners are all ablaze.

- Refrigerator doors are adjustable and can swing left or right; have yours swing *away* from the W.T., and make sure the "handled" side has at least 15 inches of counter space (unless you're a New Yorker, in which case you can skip to the end of this chapter and make do with what you have, sugar, *we understand*).

- No matter *how* small your kitchen, you'll be a happier camper with as much counter space as possible. Here's your wish list of locations: on the opening side of the refrigerator, on either side of the sink, and any zone that will multitask (i.e., act as simultaneous food prep and hors d'oeuvres sideboard).

SIZE MATTERS

Cabinets

Kitchen cabinetry typically consists of wall-mounted *wall* (upper) and *base* (lower) cabinets (see page 105 for cabinet style and finish scoop). They're sized to complement the appliances they surround. In general, they come in standard widths starting at 12 inches and can go up to 48 inches, usually in 3-inch increments. Wall cabinets are typically 12 inches deep and 30 to 42 inches tall; base cabinets are 24 inches deep and 34½ inches tall (so that with a standard 1½-inch-thick countertop, the finished height of your base cabinets will be 36 inches). You can adjust base cabinet height with either manufacturer-supplied risers or contractor-installed bases. Wall cabinets that are 12 inches tall go above refrigerators; 18-inch-tall ones above stoves. Utilitarian *ready-made* or *stock* cabinetry comes in the most basic sizes and, like its name implies, can be picked up at your big box store. Built-to-order *custom cabinetry* comes in cabinet sizes that are still fairly standardized (so technically, it's only *semi-*custom but who's to argue?), but are *much* more diverse, size-wise. Truly *made-to-measure* cabinetry (*ka-ching!*) is built to *your* very own specifications; its price tag is as hefty as the cabinetry is unique.

Design Tip

Get the built-in look on a budget in 8-foot-ceilinged kitchens by using 42-inch-tall wall cabs instead of the standard shorter ones. Butt them directly up against the ceiling. You'll love the extra shelf you gain inside the taller cabinets almost as much as you'll love how sleek and custom they look, especially in wee-willy kitchens.

For cabinetry that is not custom made, your installer will create a *filler* to fill in empty spaces between the last cabinet's edge and the wall. Fillers should match the cabinets' finish to blend in brilliantly.

Space above and below your cabinets

If you have tall ceilings, play with cabinet heights to get a chic, custom look and emphasize the height. By stacking a 12-inch-high wall cab on top of a 36-inch wall cab, for example, you get a dramatic 4 feet of cabinetry *and* gain an extra foot of storage for your Christmas ornaments where there would have been a nasty gap.

Hide wee open spaces between cabinet tops and ceilings with matching decorative trim or crown molding. If your gap measures more than 4 inches, though, have your contractor build a soffit to box the opening and make the cabinetry look built-in.

In streamlined, ultramodern kitchens, soffits are a *must*—an exposed gap between the top of your wall cabinets and the ceiling is a style no-no. Unless, of course, you have 14-foot ceilings; in that case, hang the Warhol on the wall above them and, doll, *enjoy your view!*

The standard distance between the bottom of a wall cabinet and the countertop is 15 to 18 inches. (We call the whole thing the *backsplash*, although technically a backsplash is just the 4-inch-tall vertical piece of countertop that protects the wall from splashes. More on backsplashes later.) But if you leave 20 inches of undercabinet clearance, you can have lotsa headroom for heftier countertop appliances (like that cute KitchenAid mixer you've been after).

Countertops

The standard height of countertops is 36 inches, but they can run from 34 to 42 inches. If you're tall and your existing countertops seem to stop at your crotch, stack a new countertop on top of the existing one and edge its front with matching material. If you're starting from scratch, have 42-inch-high countertops custom-made (which will also require custom base cabinets, FYI). Countertops should be at least 20 inches deep; most are 24 inches, like base cabinets. *(What a coincidence!)*

The traditional countertop thickness is 1½ inches, but amp it up to 3 inches if you just *adore* your granite or are altitude-inclined. But try not to get too carried away with the height thing unless you plan on selling your house to an NBA player or outliving your thirty-year mortgage—honey, a kitchen with extra-high countertops is a *hard* resell. On the other hand, varying your countertop height by work zones can be a plus in a chef's kitchen. Lowering a work surface to make rolling out pastry more comfortable, for example, will definitely give you a flakier crust.

Design Tip

If you can find just 3 extra feet free on a wall, install an 18- to 24-inch-deep shelf made from the same material as your countertop to create an instant desk. Either chalkboard paint or a corkboard above visibly designates the areas as *desk*. Tuck a mini tiered file cabinet (check out IKEA or art and architecture supply stores) underneath for storage.

Landing areas—clear countertop space—are crucial. Here are the numbers:

- 15 inches on the handle side of the refrigerator or on either side of a side-by-side refrigerator
- 15 inches of landing area no more than 48 inches directly opposite the fridge
- 12 inches of landing area on one side of a cooking surface, plus 15 inches on the other

Sinks and Dishwashers

The standard sink depth is 6½ inches, but the deeper your sink, the better (within reason). If your landlord has bequeathed your rental with a super-shallow sink (which 6½ inches, quite frankly, *is*), replacing it with at least an 8-inch-deep model (or a high-arching gooseneck faucet if you have the backsplash height) is a worthwhile endeavor. Because otherwise, filling up a pitcher or a large pot will become a torturous two-step process. Every. Single. Time. Here's an easy gauge: If your sink is shorter than a dinner fork standing vertically inside it, it's too shallow. Other important measurements related to your sink:

- Try to include at least a 24-inch-wide landing area to one side of the sink and an 18-inch-wide landing area to the other.
- Locate the nearest edge of the dishwasher within 36 inches of the sink.
- The dishwasher can be raised from 6 to 12 inches to accommodate countertop height.
- Leave at least 30 to 48 inches of floor space clear in front of the dishwasher to give you room to maneuver around its open door.

Seating

When shopping for stools for your kitchen, it's the *seat height* that counts. For standard 36-inch-tall countertops or island dining overhangs, counter-height stools with about a 25-inch-high seat are great.

For counters or kitchen tables above 38 inches tall, bar-height stools do the trick, with about 29- to 31-inch-high seats.

In terms of comfort, stools with upholstered seats and/or backs (tie-on seat cushions rock, too) will deliver a more comfortable seat if you'll be chilling at your countertops for lengthy periods of time (like doing eighth-grade homework). However, if it's more about breakfasting-on-the-go *chez vous*, then let stool style—and not comfort—be your guide.

It's important to consider your sight lines when selecting counter seating. In a large kitchen, stools with closed or upholstered backs are fine. For space-challenged kitchens, backless stools or those with airier, see-through backs are "transparent" and help make the room seem larger.

Banquettes

Nothing beats a corner banquette in an eat-in kitchen . . . except maybe a banquette under a row of windows. (*Note:* Banquettes take up less floor space, since *you* slide into them to sit down and not vice versa.) Your carpenter can build-in benches with flip-top seats or drawer fronts for storage, or have an upholsterer whip up a fabric-covered unit to your specs. Top wooden bases with box cushions (these have a top, a bottom, and gusseted sides); for upholstery, opt for a tight seat and upholstered back.

Create rental kitchen banquettes by aligning storage cubes or actual benches in an L-shape along corner walls. Benches should be 15 to 18 inches deep. You will want to keep your seating proportionate to the um, *generosity*, of your household's derrieres, though, so, baby, go all the way to Big 2-0 if you need to.

Padded backrests make leisurely luxuriating at your banquette irresistible *and* help keep the wall behind it clean. Create one by anchoring a long box cushion to the wall with hooks and ties, or Velcroing it so it doesn't move an inch. (*Note:* Velcroed cushions aren't reversible.) Have the cushion's top hit the top of your shoulder blades, so you can still tilt your head back with glee as you marvel at your kitchen's new creature comforts.

THE COVER-UP: STYLE AND EFFECT

Cabinets

The highest-quality kitchen cabinets are traditionally crafted of solid wood (although, honey, you *know* we just love our stainless cabs, too, now). The percentage of real wood content drops dramatically as you descend the cabinetry food chain, from MDF or chipboard shells with thin veneer fronts, to straight chipboard with melamine plastic exteriors at the bottom.

Cabinet Doors and Fronts

Cabinet doors determine your kitchen's style. If you're on a budget, you should obsess about them and little else (other

TRADE SECRET
Just a little bee in your bonnet! Many stock cabinets are surprisingly well made and feature solid wood doors. They can deliver *significantly* more quality than more stylish "budget" alternatives, although they are almost always *painfully* lacking in style. "Pre-finished" stock cabs can feature unfinished undersides, tops, and interior shelves, however, so consider lightly sanding and polyurethaning both sides of *all* bare surfaces to help prevent the wood from holding cooking odors. *

than your hardware). Here's a cheat sheet of the five most popular cabinet door styles:

If you're giving your kitchen a budget makeover, swapping out cabinet doors alone—leaving the existing cabinet frames intact—is often a great option. *Now, this might seem obvious, but...* when considering cabinet doors, keep in mind that they should complement your home's general style aesthetic. Walking into a super-modern kitchen from an English Regency dining room is nothing short of *discombobulating*.

Five popular cabinet door styles.

Recessed   Raised   Flat

Cathedral   Shaker

Now onto cabinet fronts. Cabinet fronts come in two styles: *full overlay*, with doors and drawers laid closely together so none of the cabinet frame shows underneath, and *inset* (*¼-, ½-, or 1-inch overlays*), where the doors are surrounded by visible cabinet frame. Full overlay cabinets are best for modern kitchens; choose inset styles for more traditional ones. For a look—and a price—that's somewhere in between, check out the 1-inch overlay (which actually only leaves ½ inch of frame exposed around doors).

Here are some other important cabinet rules to keep in mind:

- Indulge in clear glass-front cabinets and that cute open shelving only if your housekeeping skills are *up to snuff*! If your messiness is best kept hidden behind closed doors, make them with opaque or textured glass instead.
- For the quickest and least-painful kitchen facelift, *paint your cabinets*. It's easily done: After a thorough hand sanding, apply a coat of Aqualock primer (quiz the paint store

experts about what other superior-adhering primers will work on your particular cabinet surface) and three coats of satin oil paint in the color of your choice. (Latex paint will do in a pinch, but it won't give as hard and durable a finish.) Black painted cabinets are *divine* in a tiny city kitchen, especially since now it will look like a bar.

- To avoid appliance fronts wrecking your cabinet-front flow, choose panel-front appliances for your dishwasher and refrigerator.

SURFACES

Unless you're a recent college grad (in which case you will only ever use your kitchen to make popcorn), you'll commune with your kitchen's floors, walls, and countertops on an intimate basis. So make sure each is something you love. Or at least like a lot, if you're redoing your rental. Consider the appropriateness, sustainability, *and* style of the materials—some elements will work better than others for your needs. Granite or marble makes divine countertops, but unless you install radiant flooring underneath, it can be chilly underfoot and *fuggedaboutit!* when you drop the china and crystal. Wood floors are warm and inviting, but wood is *dreadful* as a backsplash (although a more chic look you will not find).

Countertops

There are so many countertop materials to choose from these days. Chic *and* functional are possible! But keep in mind what will work with your lifestyle. Here's what's available:

- **Laminate**—rather, *today's* version of laminate—delivers like nobody's business, and stylishly so, especially if you're on a budget. It comes in gazillions of *really good-looking* (I am *not* exaggerating!) finishes, including exotic woods, stones, and metallics.

- **Granite** is the Cadillac of countertops. It's gorgeous, feels good to the touch, and is unfazed by scratches, heat, and acids (but not grease, which is its Kryptonite). Like marble and limestone, granite is porous and requires *thorough* sealing to prevent staining. *Unlike* granite, marble and limestone scratch and stain easily and shouldn't be used for countertops, especially if you have minor-age children anywhere *near* your house (or a husband who sometimes acts like one). If your life will be listless without your white marble counters, sugar, have them sealed, sealed, and *resealed,* set your coffeemaker and whatnot permanently on clear acrylic slabs (think clear cutting boards or similar), and attack spills the *nanosecond* they occur.

- **Engineered quartz** is a composite of stone particles smooshed together, kind of like stone sausage. It's as durable as marble and stone but less delicate and costs half as much. It's manmade, so it's an ecologically friendly choice.

- **Corian** is a solid plastic material that mimics marble in looks only. It is lower maintenance in that stains—everything from red wine to burns—can be easily sanded out.

- **Butcher block**, that environmentally friendly staple of the seventies kitchen, is enjoying a huge comeback, too. Don't let their easy-to-clean-looking surfaces fool you, though, bubby: Butcher-block countertops are a chore to keep stain- and bacteria-free, and they require monthly mineral

TRADE SECRET

Dulled stone countertops are easily revived with a light pumice sanding and resealing, which is a dustless endeavor, despite the sound of it. You can do this yourself, but pros guarantee even results. ✳

oiling to maintain their luster. (Toddlers can be easier to take care of.)

Walls and Backsplashes

Clad your hardest-working walls—behind the cooktop, sink, and prep counter—in a durable and easily cleaned material. Paint and wallpaper are genius options for everywhere else. Vinyl wallpaper is a wipeable wonder, although avoid it altogether in super-steamy, ventless kitchens: Your paper and its glue will eventually go their separate ways (just like a fool and his money). Here's the skinny on disaster-proof materials for kitchen walls and backsplashes:

- **Composite tiles** are made from a mix of natural minerals and resins, are practically indestructible, and come in every color and finish imaginable.
- **Laminate sheeting** (Formica), lightweight and inexpensive resin over thin board, comes in every color under the sun. If you haven't thought much about kitchen laminates since Alice ruled the *Brady Bunch* kitchen, darling, you'll be *bowled over* to see how good they look now! And I'll repeat: Nothing else delivers as much bang for your buck.
- **Metals**, including stainless steel, copper, and aluminum, in either tile or sheet, are great for backsplashes and countertops; they're easy to cut into almost any shape and are virtually indestructible on the wall (countertops require a little more TLC).

Think of your backsplash as an opulent belt and your kitchen as a little black dress, or as Michelangelo's ceiling in your very own Sistine Chapel. It's an opportunity for style and expression in what is otherwise a pretty utilitarian environment. There may be fewer than ten basic cabinet door styles, but the possibilities for groovy, gorgeous backsplashes are *infinite*! Honey, *banish* the Boring Backsplash from your stunning kitchen.

For a sophisticated, unifying effect, extend your countertop material the full height of the backsplash wall. Cladding the rear wall alone eliminates that awkward decision about where to end the backsplash on the sidewalls . . . at the edge of the upper or lower cabinet? Hang framed pictures on your sidewalls instead, or place tall countertop appliances against them, with their rear to the sidewall.

Contrasting backsplashes look great, too—the fancier, the *bettah.* For tiles, consider a contrast field and border, a detailed pattern, or a *super*-intricate mosaic. Nine times out of ten, even the most delicate wall tiles will work marvelously on backsplashes—the biggest thing that could bump into them is a mixing bowl! For you super chefs, opt for a breeze-to-clean backsplash. In a more *decorative* kitchen (i.e., you're still single), indulge in exquisitely esoteric display elements: framed pictures or art, contrasting wallpaper, heirloom plates, or other artfully arranged collections. A mirrored backsplash is breathtaking in a small city kitchen, especially if your idea of heavy cooking is *two* Lean Cuisines instead of *one.*

Floors

Kitchen floors do need to be utilitarian. You *will* drop food and spill water on them (and that's just the tip of the iceberg if your kids are still small), but that doesn't preclude them from being statement-making and elegant! Let's consider some of your options:

- **Ceramic floor tiles** are man-made and are sturdier, less porous, and less expensive than their natural counterparts. They're available in glazed or matte finishes, and they do a fabulous job of imitating the real McCoy at a fraction of the price. Nothing is easier to clean, but you'll be grateful for the cushioning of a rubber chef's mat or something equally cushy wherever you plan on standing on the floor for long periods. Up a budget floor's style ante by arranging basic ceramic floor tiles in a snazzy pattern (see bathroom floor tile layouts for inspiration, page 134). Even alternating 12 by 12-inch tiles with rows of the same tile in a smaller size adds noticeable pizzazz underfoot.
- **Cork, linoleum, industrial rubber, and acrylic** floor tiles are low maintenance and a snap to clean. Best of all, they're warm and comfy to stand on. With the exception of acrylic tiles, these flooring materials are all derived from natural materials such as bark, oilseed, or latex, so they get the green floor award for the kitchen, too. Each comes in a gazillion patterns and colors. What's not to love?!?
- **Natural stone tiles** including slate, marble, travertine, limestone, and granite are the kings of kitchen flooring. They're more expensive than the rest but utterly worth it, stylewise, if your pocketbook permits. Natural stone floors can be cold, but radiant heating has remedied that little problem. Radiant heating, which circulates heated water through a series of cables beneath your floor, is not only more efficient than conventional heating systems, but

it also eliminates the Ugly Radiator (and its first cousin, the Unattractive Baseboard Heater). Radiant heating is truly God's gift to the ginormous country kitchen.

- **Terrazzo**, a mix of concrete and chips of marble and stone, and *concrete* itself, the latter sealed with a rubberized coating, require little maintenance other than the occasional buff and polish. Be warned: If standing for long stretches on marble is hard, then doing so on concrete can be *impossible*. So, sugar, plan your floor mats accordingly!

- **Terra-cotta** tiles, made of baked clay, are a popular choice in country, Mediterranean, or beach house kitchens. These need to be preglazed or sealed because of their porosity.

- **Wood** floors add an element of design continuity to your kitchen when you use the same selection that runs elsewhere throughout your house. From pale ash to ebonized wenge, solid wood to engineered (a top layer of hardwood mounted on a plywood base), and lacquer to oil finishes, the choices of wood flooring are many. All are warm, functional, easy to clean, and long-lasting. (See page 217 for more on wood floors.)

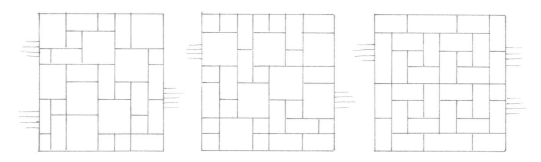

Tile flooring layout inspiration.

Range Hoods

Tons of research is available online for everything you wanted to know about kitchen appliances but were afraid to ask, so we won't go into details about those here. *However,* I *do* want to spend a minute reviewing *range hoods,* those enclosed little fans that go above your stove to help rid your kitchen of odor and smoke, because although Miele dishwashers and Viking stoves are always popular topics of discussion, range hoods never seem to be. And then, one day, you'll need to replace *yours,* and . . . what's a chef to *do*?

- Know that the professional series hood—the one with the four-figure price tag—isn't your *only* option, even if it does seem like the Hood of the Month every time you open a magazine. There are dozens of others that do the same job for a *lot, lot* less (which is why we're talking about them here!). If Mario Batali comes over to whip up a fondue every week, invest in the professional one; otherwise, go to ConsumerReports.org and read up on the look for less.

- To best get smoke and steam out of your kitchen, *avoid* the over-the-range microwave combo ("microhood"). As cute as they are (and they *are*), your hand fan actually does a better job of venting your kitchen.

- Unlike a Chanel handbag, range hoods are not one-size-fits-all. If you have wall cabinets over your range, under-cabinet hoods were designed *just* for you. They mount to the bottom of the cabinet and the ductwork attached to them conveniently routes up through the cabinet and outside through either an adjoining wall, chase, soffit, or ceiling. If you live in an apartment, you'll want the *ductless* option. If your range stands alone against a wall—*sans* cabinets above—a wall-chimney hood (it looks like a hood with a chimney attached) mounted with exposed vent stacks on the wall is the way to go. Island hoods are mounted to and vented through the ceiling. Fumes from an island range like to roam about the room, which is why it's a grand idea to buy a hood that's wider than the cooktop.

- Size matters when it comes to choosing a range hood. Pick out a little-bitty one and you will *definitely* rue the day you walked away from the stove and burned the risotto. A hood should be at least as wide as the cooking surface it hovers over.

- Manufacturers have tried to reverse the laws of gravity by directing rising smoke and fumes through ducts running beneath the floor. Surprise! Downdraft hoods *don't work*, so don't try this at home!

- The more cubic feet per minute (cfm) of air your hood can flush out of the kitchen, the better you'll be. So sugar, comparison shop! You'll also want the thermometer-friendly option that prevents the unit from overheating (and its wires melting? *Can't stand the heat in the kitchen!*) when the burners below get too hot.

- If you install the hood 18 to 30 inches above your range's burners, not only will you avoid getting a contusion every time you turn on the tea kettle, but it will draw the smoke and fumes out of the room more effectively.

- Max out the amount of smoke, heat, and unsavory food odors by venting the hood to the outside if you can.

Apartment dwellers, be sure to follow the "non-venting" instructions to get the most out of your machine.

- Metal ducting should be smooth and as large as can possibly fit your hood and inside the wall. The bigger it is, the more easily air will flow through it. And while you're at it, keep those duct runs short and as pin-straight as possible. Making smoke and fumes travel around hairpin curves ain't an easy way to get rid of them efficiently.

- Have the installer use a wall or roof cap outside of your house to prevent back drafts.

- If you're a Julia Child working your culinary finesse in your kitchen nightly, replace your filters fortnightly; otherwise, every three to six months will do, per the manufacturer's recommendation.

LIGHTING THE WAY

I champion warm, mellow lighting for almost every area of the house, but kitchens need to be brightly lit for you to see what you're doing in them (especially if you are faking knowing how to cook, which I do often). The secret to warm, inviting, kitchens is having lots of light . . . from many light sources, each on a separate switch so they can be independently operated. You'll need *general lighting* for the room; each *zone*—dining, prep, the island, and *especially the sink*, so you can *see* if your dishes are *clean*, dollface!—should have its own task light overhead; and then something a little *lounge-ier* for mellower moments or to give the room a glow when it's empty. Here's what you need to know to create the best lighting setup:

- Recessed lighting is *sheer perfection* in kitchens. You can install as many as you need to brilliantly illuminate your room without them visually cluttering up your ceiling or competing with pendant fixtures. Put them on several switches so you can light up just the zones you need. *Now this might seem obvious, but . . .* locate your bank of wall switches right by the kitchen's entrance. In most kitchens, particularly a large room, *one* surface-mounted light fixture ain't going to cut the mustard, honey. If you're relying on them as your primary light source, you'll need *several* to do the trick. Make them identical and geometrically arranged on your ceiling (like in double rows or a square).

- Pendant lights hanging above the kitchen island (which is frequently centered in the room) visually highlight and anchor the space. Hang them 36 to 48 inches above a tabletop surface so they illuminate the unit's entire length and width. Rectangular fixtures (i.e., billiard-style or similar) should be no larger than two-thirds the length of the table below. Hang multiples of smaller round fixtures (better in odd numbers if there's more than a pair) in sufficient quantities to achieve the effect.

- Keep pendants proportionate to the island or dining table they're above *and* also to the kitchen's ceiling height. When in doubt, err on the smaller size, and not vice versa (*unlike* those Beverly Hills plastic surgeons, hon). *Resist the temptation* to install 12-inch-diameter, gigantic industrial pendant lights—as adorable as they may be—unless your kitchen is very, very large, with ceilings of more than 9 feet. Otherwise they will look like fat ladies in hoop skirts swinging from your very low ceiling, about to alight on your island for a snack. The 9-inch diameters will serve you much better.

- Be conservative when combining pendant, recessed, and surface-mounted light fixtures to keep your kitchen ceiling from looking like a Christmas tree at Graceland. *One* pendant fixture or chandelier should dominate the landscape, *either* over the dining area *or* the island (and not all of the above). If you opt for other pendants in the room, they should be complementary to your superstar (same finish, similar shape or lines, etc.), but smaller-size and *much* more discreet.

- Station a lamp (or a pair!) on your countertop for an eye-level glow that is a great accompaniment to brighter lighting elsewhere in the space (like while you're eating) or to simply softly illuminate the kitchen when you're gone. Candlestick lamps are adorable in even the tiniest kitchens (*Style note:* I put a leopard-print paper shade on mine); choose beefier table lamps for larger ones. Lamps are *way* cuter than undercabinet lights, to boot.

- Sconces look great on the walls above your kitchen's dining table and help delineate the eating area, too. Position them equidistant from the zone's corners or "ends"; make sure that the sconces' bases clear—but do not tower over—a seated person's head. See how between 48 and 60 inches above the floor to the center of the back plate works for you.

- Sconces beneath the backsplash or mounted to the front of less-used wall cabinets are as cute as they can be, as long as no water will ever hit them (which is highly unlikely if you order takeout every night, so knock yourself out).

DESIGN DETAILS

Kitchens are a lot like men's suits: There aren't a whole lot of style options to choose from (Shaker style door = vented back; wenge or oak = vest or not; hardware = French cuffs + links, and you're *dressed*!), so it's the *accessories* that count. Which is good—no, it's *great*!—news, because *cabinets* can be pricey, but accessories rarely are. (Unless, of course, you're just wild about imported signed ceramics.) If you leave your kitchen unadorned, it'll still function brilliantly as Cooking Central, but why deny yourself the pleasure of spending quality time in a room that loves you back as much as you love it? Which is what I promise a styled-up, organized, and embellished kitchen will do, endlessly.

The first order of business: Color your culinary world. White kitchens *do* look fabulous, but so do brilliant red, orange, yellow, and green ones. Richly colored walls can hide a multitude of sins and add warmth, glamour, and coziness to your kitchen . . . all at once! (Now if *that's* not *delivering* for your *dollar,* stylewise, tell me what *is*!) If you can't paint your kitchen cabinets, for example, choose a wall color that highlights their existing, um, veined and glossy beauty, like a deep chocolate brown for out-of-the-box stock oak cabs. The contrast will enrich the cabinets *and* your space!

For island chic, affix something visually stimulating to the back of your cabinets (under the underhang) so it peeks out between your barstools. Get the look for less with a sheet of Formica in a contrasting bold color; or simple, oversize sheets of gold-leafed, corrugated cardboard (buy the plain paper at art or moving supply stores); pricier options include sheeted or tiled glass, or mirror or ceramic or stone wall tiles.

Extra-credit for you overachievers: Backlight your island's backside, which looks *especially amazing* if it faces out into a larger room (i.e., the living space in your eleven-million-square-foot loft). Install fluorescent tubing along the back of the cabinets, behind a sheet of glass or acrylic (or onyx or alabaster for you high rollers) screwed onto its face, so that it glows when lit. You'll need to frame out the island's edges to house the lighting and also electrify the whole shebang. Less work but almost as alluring when night falls: Install strip lights behind a lip at the overhang's front or along the upper rear of the back. (Note I did not say *anything* about neon. Don't even *think* of using neon. Do. Not. Go. There.) Consult your electrician about bulb temperature first.

Also, painting or gold-leafing the underside of your cabinets will cast a marvelous glow on the countertops below and give you a reason to smile whenever you get something out of a lower cabinet.

Go for the pretty when selecting a kitchen table—chances are, it'll be the only non-cabinet piece of furniture (oh wait, the *chairs*) in the space. Round tables work best in corner breakfast nooks (I love the classic Saarinen tulip table—or a *reasonable facsimile thereof,* if you get my drift—for modern kitchens, and classic pedestal tables for traditional ones). Check out drop-leaf tables for awkwardly shaped spots.

Chic Storage

For busy families, your kitchen really *will* serve as Command Central. (For *once* I'm not exaggerating!) To avoid clutter taking over (because it *will*, like kudzu, if you let it), plan stylish storage from the get-go:

- Use oversize chalkboards and/or fabric-covered homosote bulletin boards for schedules, notes, appointment reminders, and whatnot.
- Affix cork tiles along the walls under kitchen cabinets to use as pinboards, or horizontally hang bulletin boards, there, as well. These boards will be smaller, so you can dedicate one per child.
- School supply vendors can fabricate custom-size blackboards and corkboards, as small or as large as you need (typically up to 4 by 8 feet; if you live on the thirty-second floor of an elevator building, make sure your oversize pinboard will fit into your elevator first).
- Chalkboard painted walls are a perennial communications-center favorite. Refreshing the paint every six to nine months helps keep it pristine; yearly if you're not an obsessive type of person.
- In spite of your *best* efforts to the contrary, chances are that chaos will still reign supreme. So try to position your data center out of sight lines from other rooms.

Other Storage Tips

- Chicly hide utensils in plain sight in stylish decorative vases and/or glass vessels, lined up on your countertop (honey, I am *nuts* about hand-glazed Asian ceramics for this!). Maintain a uniformity to their look (for once I'm not opposed to *identical*) so it doesn't look like you raided a tag sale. Do the same for onions, garlic, potatoes, and fruit in cute baskets and wooden bowls. I'm stylishly storing my Vidalia onions in clear Lucite shoeboxes on my countertop these days—*j'adore!*

- Shop the bath department for long, shallow trays to store oils and spices on the countertop, too. (*Note:* Leaving oils in their original containers is fine, *especially* if you buy ones with cute labels! *I encourage* splurging a little in the name of style! And *taste!*)

ULTIMATE TRADE SECRET I cheat with my own no-frills dishwashing liquid holder—I took a clear, plastic, smaller-size original bottle, soaked and Goo-Gone'd the labels off, and have refilled it for years. I leave the lotion in its bottle, because I get the *cute ones!* ✱

- *Do* transfer dishwashing liquid, hand soap, and lotion into pretty, clear vessels or dispensers.
- If you're a cat owner faced with the small apartment/litter box conundrum, remove a door from a base cabinet in the least visible part of the kitchen and stash your kitty's box there. (*Note:* Turn this concept into a cushioned pet palace in larger, more deluxe kitchens.) If your feline needs her privacy, hang a "curtain" made from an oversize dishtowel or cute piece of fabric across the cabinet's top with Velcro, a spring rod, or ties and hooks.

Accents

- The two walls of your breakfast nook are another great spot for the two thousand family photos lingering in a box in the back of your closet.
- In a wee galley kitchen, sit a decorative box or narrow bench (painted Asian boxes and ceramic Chinese garden stools are genius), at least 18 inches tall and as narrow as 12 inches deep, at the kitchen's enclosed end as a perch.
- Show off your collection of cookie jars, *National Geographic*s, or hand-painted ceramics all in one zone on floor-to-ceiling open shelves or a freestanding étagère.

Breakfast nooks are ideal for Major Art Moments.

Design Tip

Drop-down TVs are great space savers, as are small flat screens mounted on an arm on the side of a kitchen cabinet.

- Hang framed art galore around the room, or settle on one (*a couple of*?) oversize piece(s) in a central location. (Now, sugar, this *is* a kitchen, so if you're doing any *real* work in there, choose another room for your Monets and Pollocks, and hang the stuff steam and grease won't ruin in your kitchen instead.)
- I love the unexpected drama of an *utterly breathtaking*—or brilliantly kitschy—chandelier in a kitchen. In a ratty rental kitchen, *especially.*
- *Exercise restraint.* We want your kitchen to be *brilliantly decorated*, as opposed to *clutter-filled*. (Don't worry—if you don't yet know the difference between the two, I promise you *surely will* by the time you finish this book.) Resist the urge to cover every surface, don't confuse your breakfast table with a mail sorter (*Mom, are you reading this???*), and *purge frequently!*

BATHROOMS 6

After a marvelous bedroom to soothe you to sleep at night and help you lovingly greet the new day, your bathroom is the next important room in your house, because once you've *greeted* that new day, honey, you need to *wake up* and get cracking! And your bathroom is where it all happens. I am *here to tell you* (if you haven't found this out already by yourself) that it is well nigh to *impossible* to have a great day when it begins in a bathroom bereft of style, beauty, and convenience. The best news of all, though, is that nowhere is maxing out the moolah to get a great look *less necessary* than your bathroom! Whipping up a sybaritic oasis on a dime is actually a piece of cake . . . although it might take a minute to bake, because I want you to *take your time* and not rush through this one. Linger over every delicious detail in your bath, darling, from the loo, to the lighting, to the tile and its layout, to your (preferably big) fluffy towels. Obsess about your knobs, hooks, holders, and hardware. Adoring each of these details individually will add up to a delightful, personalized spa palace that will be yours and yours alone, no matter *how* horrendous a room you started out with. Then set your beauty and grooming essentials out in stunning containers (now I didn't say *expensive*, sweetie—*love* a simple cylindrical drinking glass for the Q-tips) and charming boxes, trays, and baskets. Pay attention to every single aesthetic decision you make in your bathroom, and you'll create a room that will pay you back richly, each and every morning.

THE LAYOUT

Just because you don't live in Buckingham Palace doesn't mean you don't deserve a bathroom fit for a queen (or king)! Whatever the size, shape, or condition of what your bathroom *starts* with, don't ever settle for anything less than at least a *version* of your dream bathroom, darling. (Although renters should be a little more generous with their definition of "dream.") Here's the scoop: Much like the kitchen, the basic elements of any bathroom are the same—a tub, shower, toilet, sink, mirror, lighting, and tile. Bathroom *fixtures* are the stuff that's "fixed" (attached) to the floor, i.e., tub, shower, toilet, sink; *fittings* are the accoutrements that decorate the fixtures, i.e., faucets, tub fillers/shower bodies (that's pro jargon for the tub spigot and showerhead), towel racks, and so on. You'll also need *storage*. Start your bathroom layout by determining where your fixtures should go (and remember that moving pipes can be a pricey proposition—honey, I think plumbing might be the only recession-proof trade there is), and then work from there.

Larger Loos

If you have a roomier loo, organize the space by zones, types of activities, or his and hers. Luxuriate in your soaking tub while glancing lovingly at your shower across the room and your dressing or makeup area adjacent. Put a chaise longue in front of a window or French door so you can recline in splendor and read a book or make phone calls in your fluffy terry cloth bathrobe after you brush your teeth on the weekends. (And, bubby, call me first so I can let you know just how jealous I am of your gargantuan space.)

The walk-in, oversize shower is one of the grooviest trends around, and you shouldn't even *try* to live without one if you have a Texas-size bath. Extend your shower's length to at least 8 feet (and up!); make the width as wide as you can, and be *sure* to include at least one window in the space for natural light if possible. Install showerheads at both ends of the setup (his and hers!) and a little handheld number on a tiled pedestal in the middle of the space (try dead center or at the center of the rear sidewall) for hosing down the dog. If you have sufficient empty space surrounding your shower, a glass wall or shower curtain isn't necessary. Add a marble saddle at the entrance, make the shower a step down, or *really*

TRADE SECRET
Design pros and contractors frequently refer to bathrooms as "water closets," since loos were first located in small, closet-like spaces. You'll often see bathrooms designated on plans as "W.C."s to help differentiate them from B.R.s, so your tile doesn't get installed in your *bedroom*. In the strictest technical sense today, though, W.C. actually refers to a *toilet*, although almost only toilet vendors call them that. *Fascinating, isn't it!!!* ✱

Create the Ultimate Shower Experience in Texas-size baths.

angle the shower's floor for maximum drainage. Speaking of which, don't forget floor drains at each zone to prevent your Ultimate Shower Experience from turning into the Great Flood.

If you really want a grand loo, go for the Old World luxury of a private W.C. within your bathroom, and install your toilet in its own little doored space. Make this a *vented* space, though, so air circulates; air-cooled is great if you have central air. And as obvious as this seems, don't forget to light the space, either via overhead or a pretty wall sconce. Avoid stinting on square footage for your private W.C.—(A), you don't want to feel claustrophobic, and (B), you'll need floor space for a basket or two of magazines!

Smaller Loos

Generally you can create the illusion of space in a small bathroom by using see-through materials wherever possible and leaving your floor uncluttered: Think glass for the shower stall, heavy-duty transparent shower curtains for the tub, wall-mounted sinks and shelving/storage units. For medium-size bathrooms, use glass or half-walls—or a combination of both: a tiled half-wall behind your tub with a to-the-ceiling glass partition on top—to separate spaces.

Separating the toilet from the bath is a great idea in a small W.C., even if the only thing that's standing between the two is your vanity-sink combo. It makes the space more efficient, keeps you from bumping your elbow when brushing your teeth, and helps prevent splattering H_2O all over the wall when washing up.

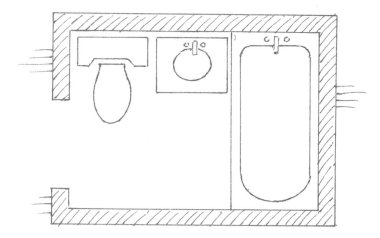

Station your sink in the middle of bite-size loos.

Layout Tips for Every Bathroom

- All shower and W.C. doors should always swing 90 degrees out, in case you ever need to leave in a hurry, darling (like when accidentally doused with scalding water, which can happen to the best of us).

- Have towels a hand's reach away from wherever you need to use them (i.e., sink and tub or shower). Now, this may sound obvious, but . . . if there isn't room for a towel bar immediately adjacent to your shower, install a hook or hooks there instead. (While we're at it, darling, here's a rule of thumb: A towel bar or rack should hold at least two folded towels. If you love oversize towels—and, sugar, you should; *bath sheets rule!*—drying yourself off with anything smaller than a bath sheet is not only inelegant but will also make you feel as big as a house! Because those little Barbie-size bath towels can be teensy!—install pairs of longer (24-inch) towel bars instead of the standard 18-inchers.

THE COVER-UP: STYLE AND EFFECT

Unless you are married to a plumber (*smart you!*) or dug oil in the backyard last week, relocating your fixtures is generally a pricey enough proposition to not even *entertain* the thought of doing so. So when you're thinking about tricking out your loo, focus on the elements that are easily changed and come in infinite choices: your bathroom's walls, flooring, fittings, lighting, hardware, and accessories. And we're off!

Walls

You have some choices when it comes to your walls in the bathroom.

Wallpapered walls for your loo are the cat's meow and look fabulous, too. The secret to successfully maintaining them is to open the door immediately after showering (or leave it open while you do) and opening the room's window (if you have one) afterward, too, to allow it to dry out perfectly every time.

If you're nervous about wallpaper, paint your bathroom walls in a gorgeous color. (*Note:* Bathrooms don't need to be painted in an eggshell or satin finish unless you plan on hosing your walls down every day [your painter won't believe me, but *you* should!]). Almost always, a matte latex finish is *fine!* And a *washable* matte latex finish is even better.

Either way (wallpaper or paint), the walls surrounding your bathtub (we call them the tub surround, just to be cute and confusing) should always be tiled if you'll ever be splashing at least one little drop of water in the zone on a regular basis. In fact, tile in general is a bathroom's best friend and can be used abundantly to a dazzling effect!

Bathroom Tiles

"Roman baths," featuring floor-to-ceiling tiled walls, can be *lovely* to look at, but know that they can *also* be hard to heat in the winter and clammy in the summer if insufficiently ventilated. More practical—and equally stylish—are bathrooms with a tile wainscot on the walls (see below) with full tiling around the tub.

Nothing says chic more cheaply than 3 by 6-inch white ceramic subway tiles. Run them 4 feet up the wall above the floor all around the room (don't forget a cove base tile at the floor and a bullnose or other decorative finishing tile at the upper edge) for a tile wainscot. Completely tile the three walls that surround your tub (from the upper edge of the tub to the ceiling), and then that ceiling, too. Edge the tub surround with a bullnose or other finishing tile that matches the top of the adjacent wainscoting. If you're squeezing every penny (and who isn't!?!?), ignore the wainscoting and just tile the tub surround. *Don't* not tile the ceiling of your tub surround as a cost-saving measure—it will cost you exponentially more in style than in dollars.

You can add a "belt" of contrasting tiles about halfway up the walls of your tiled tub surround for easy-on-the-wallet visual drama in a white-tiled loo. (See how 22 inches above the tub looks *chez vous* for positioning, but trust your own eye on this one.) Some of my favorites are five rows of 1-inch glass or ceramic tiles (the top and bottom rows of the "belt" can contrast the center three), three rows of subway tiles in a contrast color (or a belt of two contrast tiles with the white tile of the field between them), or a ready-made tile border that's preassembled by the vendor. Be sure that the contrast tiles

Dress up your tiled tub surround with a belt of gorgeous mosaics.

you select are the same thickness as the field tile. On the side walls, end the belt just before the bullnose border.

Even the most boring tiles look better when laid out in eye-catching patterns. Subway tiles in particular should always be laid in what bricklayers call a "running bond" pattern. Here it is with other inspiration for you from the wonderful world of bricks (tons more, as always, online, doll).

Lay subway tile out in a running bond pattern, like this.

Creative floor tile layouts to be inspired by.

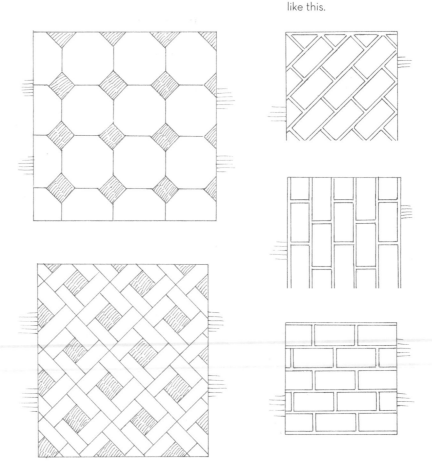

Another terrific tile choice for bathrooms is 12-by-12 floor and wall tiles. They are the Gap T-shirts of bathroom décor. To gild this lily, lay them out in a visually interesting pattern (i.e., not straight-run squares), even if it's just on the diagonal. Adding contrasting tiles or alternating sizes of the same tile also adds zing.

Glass tiles make simply stunning decorative inserts on floors, but resist the temptation to *swathe* your bathroom floor in them, no matter how swell they look—these tiles are too delicate to be trampled on all day. Shower floors, on the other hand, get a lot less wear (and even then, it's bare feet), so indulge in them there.

Design Tip

Add character to stoned-up bathrooms by using polished stone on the floors and honed stone on the countertops, or vice versa, for a richer, more complex look.

When grouting white floor tiles, I'll confess that the white tile/white grout combo looks *mahvelous*! But, baby, they'll need more tending to than a cranky two-year-old. Which is fine for the truly anal (I'll confess—that's me! I couldn't resist!) or super-neat folks with tiny, tiny loos. Everybody else should pretty much stick to the palest gray (or darker) for grouting white floor tiles.

Baseboards

Bathroom walls need baseboards, too! For tiled walls, the baseboard should match the walls; on walls without tile, the baseboard should match the floor. Tiled floors should have a stone baseboard made of the same material as the floor. Cove base tiles (they slope at the floor) are beautiful if they're available in your wall tile; if not, run the wall tile straight to the floor (which, BTW, also looks more modern and sleeker). Many ceramic floor tiles come with a matching base, but if not, create one by cutting floor tiles into smaller pieces of at least 4 inches tall. The 3-inch ready-made tile bases are fine, too, although not quite as adorable. If you're going for the real deal—genuine marble or stone—have a 4- to 7-inch baseboard cut out of the same goods as your floor and the upper edge finished with either a straight or ogee (curvily stepped) bevel.

Nothing is more luxurious (and attractively so, to boot) than under-floor radiant heating in a bathroom that you own (not rent). (See page 112 for the skinny.) Towel warmers, multitaskers that they are, also stylishly heat their surrounding space. Baseboard heaters are, um, passable under duress. Whatever you choose, though, unheated or barely heated bathrooms are a design no-no . . . and one of the first things contractors and developers will try to leave you with these days. So watch out for those little '60s-style, wall-recessed electric coil heaters that every Holiday Inn proudly featured back in the day, which (*trade secret!*) are nothing short of a builder's sorry excuse for saving a buck without passing on the savings to you. Make a point of checking out bathroom heating if you're buying new construction and insisting on baseboard heaters at the very least.

Sinks and Vanities

Pedestal sinks, cute as they may be, work best in small baths, guest baths, and the bachelor lairs of men with minimal grooming habits. If you need to store anything other than a tube of toothpaste and an extra roll of TP in your loo, though, put your sink into a vanity (or commandeer a nearby closet for storage).

Remember, any beautiful chest or table can be turned into a bathroom vanity. (See page 77 for the scoop.) Floating vanities—wall-mounted and really clearing (not grazing) the floor—are *geeenius* in the tiniest loos beneath wall-mounted sinks. Camouflage visible plumbing by installing shelves cut to accommodate the pipes. Simple open-backed cube storage units are divine candidates, in combos proportionate to the width of your sink.

Kitchen cabinets make *awesome* vanities, too. If you're a lucky devil with more than 36 inches available for your vanity space—think double sinks or multiple vanities—then, dollface, *be* a kitchen cabinista in your W.C.! Ask your friendly kitchen planner to whip up a design today.

But ready-made vanities have never looked better, so, honey, take the path of least resistance and avail yourself of one that suits your style today. Built of MDF (medium-density fiberboard), richly stained or painted, topped with gorgeoso faux marble built-in sinks, and rarely clocking in at more than $150, they're easy and affordable upgrades, a worthwhile investment even for renters.

You can change the knobs on ho-hum vanities for more pizzazz. It's like adding souped-up buttons to a bargain basement suit! Nail card-catalog pulls to the fronts of stationary drawers; if you're stymied finding a hot little number to replace two-holed handles, consider installing double sets of identical knobs (one per hole, with a smaller one above a larger one). Shamelessly claim you did it on purpose because it looks so irresistibly chic.

Skirting the issue is the quickest fix for unsightly sinks of all sizes, whether or not there's a vanity below. Attach your skirt using Velcro affixed to the perimeter of the sink itself if wall mounted, and at the top of the vanity beneath the countertop if not. For weightier skirts, use a clear, water-based sealant as glue (hello, hardware store). Modernists, keep your skirts tailored; *pour les romantiques*, go for frillier gathers and ruffles.

A wall-to-wall sheet of mirror looks fabulous above a niche-based vanity or double sink. The mirror should touch the back of your backsplash and extend all the way up to the ceiling line. Mount your lighting directly onto the mirror (have the electrical gem box for the light fixture installed first so the mirror vendor can cut out holes in the right location).

Dress up the tired sink you can't replace with a cute, tailored skirt.

Nothing visually expands a space better than large expanses of mirror (while also reminding you to watch it at the cookie jar, too).

Bathtubs

Replacing bathtubs in city apartments is a Herculean task (both labor- and walletwise) that is seldom worth undertaking. Reglazing them is infinitely easier both ways. Pros spray a light paintlike epoxy that generally lasts between five and ten years, which takes about a day to cure after application. Be sure to avoid abrasive cleansers on reglazed surfaces afterward, though—one dose of the scratchy stuff will leave scratch marks that can't be removed.

Medicine Chests

Medicine chests should be recessed. Without exception. Anything else is just plain tacky! If your loo comes with a surface-mounted number, sugar, it has *got to go*!!!! Replace it with a recessed one (the cabinet's frame should compliment your décor) or a simple clip-mounted plate-glass mirror, no smaller than 24 by 30 inches above a 24-inch sink ($20 and less at your big box store).

Medicine chests are one of the few things in design where bigger is almost always better (as long as they are recessed!). You'll adore the convenience of tucking an oversize one (up to 60 inches long—that's *5 vertical feet*—of storage, dollface! Off to Costco you go!) discreetly behind your bathroom's door. Having it as a floor-length mirror almost makes up for its (unfortunately fairly pricey) cost. Having one, period, if you installed a pedestal sink, will *save your sanity.*

If you don't have a medicine chest, opt for style over substance and store your grooming essentials atop your toilet tank in a lovely long box or low-edged basket, or on a tray.

Fittings

The quest for perfect fittings starts with choosing their finish. You want the finishes for all the fittings in your loo either to match or complement each other (matchy-matchy has a moment, at last!). Chrome and nickel are the white metals; nickel, the more expensive of the pair, has a richer, deeper luster that more closely approximates (untarnished) silver but requires regular polishing to maintain. Chrome, which is actually short for chromium, was introduced as a carefree alternative to the once-ubiquitous nickel in the 1940s, and wipes clean with a rag. Design *cognoscenti* will be mortified to hear this, but *I love chrome* because *who* has time to *polish their faucets!?!?!* Mixing nickel and chrome in your W.C. is fine (don't ask! don't tell!), but not side by side because you *can* tell the difference when they're close together. Brass fittings look great in traditional bathrooms; copper and wrought-iron style finishes add a more rustic touch.

After finishes, you're on to shape. Curvier or straighter-lined? Arching gooseneck faucets or sleeker ones? English traditional or streamlined ultramodern? More than anything else in a basic little loo (except for the lighting), it's the fittings that will make the biggest style statement in the joint. And for *once*, it's an affordable statement to make, no matter what style you choose—there are super-chic options at every price point.

SIZE MATTERS

Here are the measurements you need to know for a perfectly balanced bathroom:

- Tiled wainscoting should end about 48 inches above the floor. This is a question that decorators get asked frequently, so we're starting off with that!
- Think of your mirror and the vanity or sink below as a *unit*, and scale them appropriately to each other. The mirror over a vanity should always approach or equal the width of the unit below, and vertically fill as much space as possible between the top of the sink and the bottom of any light fixtures mounted above. (If light fixture-less, make that below

the ceiling line, only feel free to have a little more open space vertically in this case.) See page 80 for illustration.

- Try to keep at least 12 inches between the tub and any adjacent fixtures (i.e., toilet or sink). Although if you live in New York, you will find this virtually impossible to do.
- Allocate a minimum of 36 inches square for a stall shower. Sugar, I'll tell you that that is *still* a bit cramped for my liking, and if you can go larger, you definitely should. You want your shower roomy, and you *also* want it large enough so the water doesn't spray out onto the neighboring floor when you first enter it to turn it on. Don't forget a tiled recess or little step to put your things on or rest your foot while shaving your leg.
- Toilets range in depth from about 27 to 32 inches, which means they require at least 4½ feet between the toilet wall and the opposite one. (Honey, this explains why most NYC bathrooms are exactly 5 feet square, which is also the length of the average bathtub.) You'll need 30 to 36 inches of wall space to accommodate the tank's width.
- The center of a sink ideally should be at least 18 inches from an adjacent wall and its front edge at least 28 inches from the wall it faces. *Now* you know why it makes sense to put the sink *between* the toilet and the tub in tiny little loos, bubby.
- When double-sinking, allow yourself at least 5 feet of counter space (and 6 is better).

LIGHTING

Although I am the national poster child for rich, warm rooms softly lit by lamplight, *surprise!* the bathroom isn't one of them.

Bathrooms should be brightly lit, and the brighter the better, especially as one, *ahem*, ages. The secret is putting all your loo lighting on separate switches so you can adjust the light according to what's going on in there at the moment (bubble bath, putting on your face, number one or number two). See the light perfectly with a glow coming from both above and along both sides of the mirror (the better to *see* you with, my pretty!), something in the center of the room for overall illumination, and then a recessed waterproof fixture above your bathtub (so you won't be soaping up in total darkness once you close your shower curtain) or shower stall (ditto *sans* curtain).

Above-the-sink overhead lighting that casts a shadow on you when you're standing beneath it will make putting on makeup a nightmare, girlfriend. As a rule, overhead fixtures positioned about 24 inches out from the wall work to avoid dark shadows, but try this out with a lamp held above you *chez vous* to determine what best works for you.

I am *crazy* about recessed lighting for bathrooms. Especially when they are on dimmers. And wall sconces, too, especially in awkwardly laid out loos, where a single wall sconce—try centering one above the toilet—can often do the job of side-of-the-mirror lighting. Don't end your sconce search in the bath department, though—many of the ones for living rooms, exteriors, and halls work well in W.C.s, too. However, if you have seven people sharing one bathroom, stick to the more moisture-friendly ones for bath.

If you have a Texas-size bath, indulge in cute candlestick or boudoir lamps. Place a pair along a dressing table or even atop your (endless . . . *sigh*) vanity for a sumptuous champagne-and-bubbles glow, or to softly illuminate the room at night.

DESIGN DETAILS

Presentation is nine-tenths of the law! Store grooming necessities—no matter how banal—attractively in clear vessels, small vases, little baskets, and cute boxes. Group brow and nail grooming things together in shot glasses or wee bud vases. House perfume collections on pretty trays; scour the bed, bath, kitchen, dining, office, and gift departments for your collection and flea markets and thrift stores for vintage finds. If you're short on space, stash your stuff stylishly in stackable wooden CD units from IKEA or office supply stores. Drape a pretty textile over their tops (*love* fancy powder room towels or organic linen weaves for this) to unify the grouping, and then use the top surface as a station for makeup, brushes, and grooming essentials.

Here are more details to remember:

- Art *does* belong in the bathroom. (Although not your Picasso, which should grace a less humid space.) So go ahead and fill the walls with framed beauties, but *do* open a win-

Chicly store grooming essentials in a stylish tank top tray.

dow or leave the door open or ajar while showering to help keep moisture at bay,

- *News flash!* Shower curtain liners are not permanent (and neither are they pricey!). Replace them every six to nine months, or before that if they begin to look mildewy. My mother has had one of hers for at least twenty years. *Mom, are you reading this?* Once you get a new one, dollface, know that simply pulling it closed after every shower helps avoid mildew buildup in your shower curtain's creases. If you can, hang your shower curtains as close to the ceiling as possible, leaving about a half inch clear to accommodate the tops of the curtain rings. This will make the ceiling in your bathroom look more Empire State Building and not Land of the Seven Dwarfs. Find extra-long shower curtains and liners online or have a local seamstress whip one up for you in a fabric you adore.

- Avoid the five-piece plush bathroom set at all costs. Do. Not. Go. There.

- Think out of the box when shopping for bath mats. Any appropriately sized area rug works, so choose a pretty one that feels good underfoot and is easy to wash.

- An oversize area rug is the *perrrrfect* quick fix for covering up ugly tile.

- *Splurge on the most luxurious towels you can (or can't) afford.* Darling, it's *you* that's swaddling yourself in them every time water hits you! Having nice towels is like wearing nice underwear— it's a secret pleasure that makes you feel *maaaaaaahvelous* every time it touches your body. (And, sugar, your towel alone touches *all* of you, *n'est-ce pas*?) At the end of the day, two sets is all a body needs, to boot: clean and dirty. So don't stint in the Turkish towel department; you deserve it.

- Install hooks on the rear wall of your tub surround to hold your washcloths and shower caps. You can have fancy ones professionally installed by a handyman (otherwise they *will* eventually fall down, unless you have a way with toggle bolts), or use the suction-cupped ones. Affixing them to the wall with waterproof silicone adhesive also is a nifty trick; be sure to let dry twenty-four to forty-eight hours before using.

- Most of all, remember that bathrooms require more ventilation than any other room in your house, or yours will eventually feel like Miami in the middle of August. Keep humidity at bay by opening your bathroom window daily or leaving the door open as often as you can (and *always* for at least an hour or two after showering).

FOYERS AND ENTRYWAYS

They send you off to greet the world every morning and say *welcome home* every night. The first space you see when you walk through a front door, foyers and entryways set the tone for the subsequent psychological experience of your home and the way it's lived in. Think of them as style ambassadors that make an indelible first impression, which repeated coming and going further intensifies. And if you're the type to insist on sneaking through the garage, sugar, I'm not letting you off the hook, either! *Mudrooms* should be just as cute (although not as elegant)! Well-designed foyers—and mudrooms!—should fulfill three specific goals: to make a style statement about who you are as a household and how you like to live; to be a "depressurizing chamber" that subliminally signals your retreat from the hectic, harsh outer world into your nurturing inner sanctum; and to stylishly (*STYLE-ISH-LY!!!!*) equip you to enter and exit your aerie in an organized fashion (think keys, mail, briefcases/totes, etc.).

THE LAYOUT

Above all, foyers and entryways are high-traffic zones that not only serve as points of entry, but are also typically high-traffic zones that connect the living spaces of your home. Traffic flow is important in every room of your house, but doubly important in your foyer, especially if it is short on space. Give your furniture layout a test drive by walking through the space with packages, bags, moving children, strollers, boisterous pets, absent-minded plumbers and husbands, etc.

No foyer is finished without the following: a protective something on the floor for wiping feet (see page 151 for more on rugs), a table to put mail and keys on, and a mirror for guests to give themselves a final once-over as they enter and for you to admiringly glance at yourself one last time before you leave at the beginning of the day. (If you have a powder room, you can skip the mirror and hang dramatic art instead. Unless you are as vain as I am, sugar, in which case make sure the mirror is *large*.)

If you don't have a coat closet, add an umbrella stand and standing coat rack. (Don't forget to put the coat rack away when the weather warms up, doll.) Wall hooks look great in multiples, like three or five lined up in a row, spaced at least 8 inches apart, but try to keep them in casual spaces like mudrooms. And oversize vases from the garden store make spectacular umbrella stands (I am crazy about the clear glass cylinders).

In roomy entryways, a round table floating in the center of the room looks amazing, particularly with a dramatic floral arrangement on top. If you have space, add a chair or a bench along a wall or under the stair for guests to sit on and remove their shoes and where you can toss bags, purses, coats, etc. before putting them away.

Awkward Spaces

If your foyer is awkwardly shaped, focus on the architectural details, instead. Add some if there aren't any, and upgrade your space visually using your vast decorator talent. Consider swapping out dull doors for niftier ones with more trim, bells, and whistles, adding a chair rail or wainscoting, or even paneling your walls (real or faux—don't ask, don't tell!).

If you live in a small, foyer-less apartment, create a faux-entry by stationing a chair, small table, or bench as near as you can to the front door. I manage the tight squeeze in my own apartment with an antique Japanese trunk. Whatever you use should be at least chair seat height (17 to 19 inches tall).

Home dwellers who walk straight into the living room from the front door can create a faux foyer by cleverly using a folding screen (see Living Rooms, Chapter 1). This trick assumes at least 4 feet of empty wall space immediately adjacent to the door, though, to avoid bruising your knees banging into furniture every time you walk through your door.

The essentials of a stylish
and functional foyer.

SIZE MATTERS

Most foyers do not afford much space, so every inch counts!
Again, some kind of table is a must. If you have the space
and opt for a round table in the foyer, its diameter should
be proportionate to the space—48 inches and up is lovely
for large spaces; 36 to 38 inches better for smaller ones. As
pretty as a center table is, though, having sufficient space

clear around its perimeter is a must. Anything less than 4 feet clear all around is visually skimpy, not to mention awkward to navigate.

Creating a Big Splash in Teeny, Tiny Foyers

Turn tiny foyers into charming jewel boxes that ooze with warmth and welcome (rather than induce depression and claustrophobia, which is what they tend to do if you don't fix them up). Chinese consoles are the narrowest tables around and work with any style décor. Create an elegant, custom tabletop by mounting an 8- to 10-inch-deep shelf (how wide is your space?) on purchased brackets (find utilitarian ones at hardware stores, fancier decorative brackets at supply stores online) or corbels (*corbels* are fancy decorative brackets— *j'adore*). If your shelf is made of a heavy material like marble, you'll most likely need a center bracket, too. Station a slender candlestick lamp with a pretty shade, a narrow tray for keys (check out the bath department for tank top trays and soap dishes that will be perfectly sized, ditto for the desktop accessories aisle), a framed picture or two (vary the sizes), a fragrant candle, and if you have room, an orchid (go ahead and make it a fake one if your foyer doesn't get sunlight; just be *sure* to dust it regularly so it doesn't get scary looking, honey).

Foyer Flooring

Area rugs can look great in some foyers . . . and like flying carpets temporarily garaged until the next trip in others, they stand out so much. As a rule, the more furniture you have

Build a shelf to serve as a table in the foyer-less apartment.

actually sitting on a rug in a foyer, the more appropriate a rug is for the space. I love center medallions and painted geometrical motifs in squarish-shaped foyers. These are great in contrast materials if you have a marble or stone floor or either stained or painted-on hardwood floors. If you have a fabulously designed floor, then *definitely* avoid an area rug on top of it.

If you'd prefer the barefoot, open-and-breezy feeling of a rugless foyer, it'll suffice to have a simple mat the width of the front door both outside *and* inside your entrance. The inside one can be either fancy and decorative (i.e., a real rug) or utilitarianly chic (because technically, the outdoor mat does the heavy lifting).

THE COVER-UP: STYLE AND EFFECT

Your foyer is a new visitor's first exposure to both your personal and decorating style, so really *think* about what you want yours to say when planning its décor. It's a space that doesn't have very much furniture in it, so every single thing you put in there—from your table to the art on the wall to the receptacles and trays you put out for keys and mail—should be nothing less than adorable. The *unfortunate-looking* has nothing to hide behind (as it sometimes can quite successfully do in a more-cluttered space), so off with its head, my pretty!

But also remember, your foyer and mudroom can be the most heavily trafficked spaces in your house, depending on your household constituency. If you have very young children, yours will overflow with strollers and oversize diaper bags. You'll want to emphasize access, durability, and cleanability. If you have school-age kids who seem to be training for fifteen Olympic sports and have the gear to prove it, attractive storage should be at the top of your shopping list. If it's just you and the dog, import stunning hooks from Paris for Baxter's leashes and then style your foyer up the wazoo because nobody will be bumping into anything but you.

Max out the drama on your foyer walls, but take into consideration the rooms that unfold around them, which the wall treatment should complement but not perfectly match. If you're using multicolored patterned wallpaper, for example, the wallpaper's colors could include the wall colors of the visible adjacent rooms. If you walk into a rich, darkly hued room past the foyer, then keep the entrance's walls warm but lighter-toned (i.e., a taupe foyer leading to a chocolate brown room); the same is true in reverse (a chocolate foyer leading to a paler beige or yellow room).

LIGHT THE WAY

Make sure your foyer lighting, whether ceiling- or wall-mounted or atop a table, is nothing less than gorgeous. For almost every other room in the house, unobtrusive works for ceiling fixtures, but your entrance lights should be *statement-making*. And also on dimmers. Here are some options:

- Pendant lanterns look great as ceiling fixtures in smaller-size entrances. Match your style and shape ("lantern" describes any fixture hanging from the ceiling with one enclosed bulb at the end of a cord or chain, not just a classical style of light, as opposed to chandeliers, which have multiple arms) to your space. If your foyer is large enough, consider a pair.
- If space is tight, try a pair of wall sconces as your main light source. It's okay to mount them on just one wall if your room is tiny.
- The glow of lamplight gives your foyer warmth and coziness that you should never do without. Put either a single lamp or a pair of taller candlestick lamps on your entrance table, and feel free to turn off the overhead and leave these perpetually on when you're home. (I do!) To accommodate lamps on a center table, you'll need a plug receptacle in the floor; have an electrician install one for you. Try out the wattage in your lightbulbs until you get just as much—or as little—glow as you need.

DESIGN DETAILS

It's all in the simple details when it comes to foyers. Here are some ideas for fabulous finishes:

- Sit a pretty tray on your foyer table to hold the day's mail. Put a smaller one next to it for keys. Add a third for sunglasses and gloves. Or use a larger tray or two and put smaller items in vases, glasses, or bowls on top of the trays.

- If you are mail-averse and clutter-prone, station a laundry-size basket or storage box beneath your table to throw all your mail in. Sugar, be sure the basket itself is stunning, since it will truly be holding a *big mess*. Make yourself empty it at least once a month (since you'll need to pay your bills then, anyway). If your table is large enough, opt for two or three identical baskets underneath. Try turning them short- and then long-side-out to see which works better with your setup.

- Turn to Ralph Lauren (who admittedly does the best job in town), decorating magazine pictures, and design blogs and Web sites for inspiration on how to breathtakingly style your foyer table. Don't forget your vase of flowers or an orchid or two! (*Note*: If you have a foyer with super-tall ceilings, then your flowers should be tall and stately, too. Cherry blossoms, dogwood, and even low-lying branches trimmed from trees in the backyard are all amazing-looking options.)

- Be sure your space smells as good as it looks: Don't forget the scented candle (burn them often—they're not just for guests, they're for you!), aromatic sticks (don't forget to turn them over at least weekly), and potpourri (which needs dusting or it starts looking funny).

- Remember to keep your foyer table (and your foyer, while we're at it, honey) tidy, unless you want to give the impression that you don't care. Because we know you *do*!

BASEMENTS

8

Basements are almost always the stepchildren of a house, Siberias for misfit furniture and forlorn belongings. But if you think about your basement not for what it is ("What! A! Dump!" to paraphrase Bette Davis), but what it *could* be—an extra room that runs the *entire* footprint of your home—then, *hellooo! Now* it's a whole new story! The best part of which is that modern basements have transcended the rumpus room and gone where basements had never ventured before . . . sugar, we're talking subterranean chic!

Depending on their size, style, and location, basements make excellent spaces for kitchens (especially summer kitchens if there's an exit out to the backyard garden), billiard rooms, libraries, home offices, gyms, and spas. (You'll notice that I *didn't* say laundry room—there's no reason to *ever* schlep up and down a flight of stairs just to wash your towels; today's washer and dryer belong near your bedroom, where your clothes actually live.) If transforming your basement into a livable space is out of the question because it is perpetually wet, find the source of the dampness and eliminate it once and for all. (Don't forget to check for mold behind your walls, especially if it's been damp for a while or the wetness was extensive.) Dahling, when you realize that your tricking out your basement is like increasing your square footage without actually having to construct an addition, you'll wonder what ever *took* you so long to do it!

THE LAYOUT

A basement just may be the hardest space to lay out in a house, since it's home to the structure's foundation, supports, and mechanical innards, none of which can be easily moved or altered, so you'll have to be clever and work around them. If your basement is one big open space (I do hesitate to use the word *loft-like*, but wouldn't it be lovely if we could?), erect Sheetrock walls to create one or several smallish rooms around its perimeter to house the furnace, oil burner, and other HVAC-related items, and reserve the center open space for living. Make enclosed storage part of your floor plan, too. Be *sure*, however, to avoid creating a rabbit warren of small rooms:

small rooms + low ceilings = a sure recipe for claustrophobia. Instead, divide your basement great room's space visually into zones according to use, just as you would a large living or great room upstairs. (See Living Rooms, page 2).

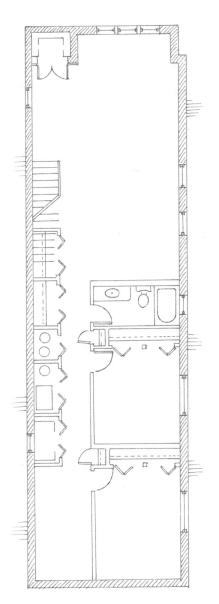

A great-looking basement layout for the townhouse-shaped home.

This one works for
a suburban manse.

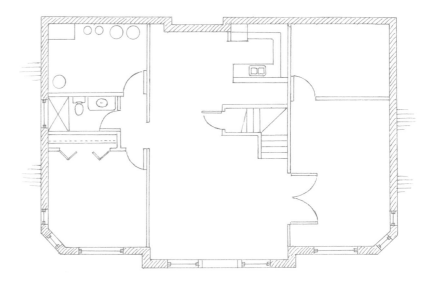

When laying out your new basement space, keep sight lines in mind. If you live in a smaller house, then a great room with one or two small storage spaces along one or two walls is a great layout option. A larger footprint is perfect for dividing into more rooms; pay close attention to window locations when delineating the room space—each room needs to get some natural light. Transoms (small framed glass inserts at the top of walls or above doors) and side lights (framed glass inserts along the sides of doors) can help bring light into nonwindowed areas from adjacent rooms, using either clear or frosted glass.

One of my favorite rooms in a basement? A bathroom or half bath. Installing a bathroom or half bath in your basement means you never have to walk up a flight of stairs to pee in the middle of a movie. (Ladies, it's also a perfect place to hand-launder *all* your lingerie at once and leave it dangling *all over the place* for a whole week without feeling guilty.)

THE COVER-UP: STYLE AND EFFECT

The three hardest parts of stylishly finishing your basement are creating an interesting but functional floor plan, maximizing ceiling height, and bringing in additional light from outside. Having to work around its fixed features (columns, beams, pipes, furnace, etc.) doesn't make the job any easier, either. The good news is that there is *always* an attractive solution to any visual nightmare—if you can't eliminate an eyesore, then camouflage it. Here are some groovy solutions to common basement design dilemmas:

Basement Design Dilemma: Nastiness Underfoot

Try as you might to prevent it from happening, the truth is that your basement floor is likelier to see more moisture than any other surface in your house. So anticipate this when choosing your flooring. *Lucky you*—water-resistant flooring has never looked better! Whatever you opt to do, know that leaving a concrete basement floor bare is *not an option*! A concrete floor is the saddest floor in town. *Laminate hardwood* is heaven-sent for basement floors. It's warp proof, perfect for a room that is vulnerable to moisture. Be sure to choose laminate (which is plastic at the end of the day) and NOT prefinished hardwood (which is actually a wood veneer over plywood). Today's laminate flooring comes in dozens of widths and colors and finishes and does a mind-blowingly good job of approximating the real thing.

- **Ceramic tile** is just what the doctor ordered, as is vinyl tile, too, especially for gyms. Avoid marble or other natural

TRADE SECRET
Decorative sleight of hand is a designer's stock in trade, so don't feel guilty about resorting to it. And there's always a fix! *

stone tiles unless you find mausoleums fun places to visit or have always aspired to live in a morgue.

- **Indoor/outdoor carpeting** has moved *waaaaaaay* beyond the Astroturf days of yore and now comes in breathtakingly beautiful faux wools and sisals. Acrylic/nylon blend indoor/outdoor carpets with interesting textures are perfect for basement wall-to-wall or area rugs. As a rule, anything that can be used outdoors will work beautifully in your basement. NEVER indulge a desire to put down wool carpet in the basement, even if you *can* afford to replace it frequently. (Save that money for your dream kitchen, sugar, where you'll get a *much* better return on your investment.)

- **Sheet vinyl flooring and vinyl tiles, either residential or commercial grade**, are the cheapest options for basement flooring, and they will resist water like Noah's ark. You'll be delighted to see the stylish options available in both (my favorite tiles are the ones that do an adorable job of replicating wood parquet). If you're going for super-utilitarian chic, lay two or three colors of commercial-grade squares out in a fun geometric pattern like a checkerboard, racing stripes, diamonds, etc.

- If you're laying floor material in a striped pattern—which, by the way, is a great way to add pizzazz to a windowless room bereft of detail—pay attention to the direction the stripes run. It is generally but not always best for the stripes to run widthwise rather than lengthwise in a small room, to avoid that bowling alley effect. Exceptions depend on the location of windows and doors, as well as how your furniture is laid out in the space. For example, if the entrance to a rectangular basement is on a short wall, run the stripes lengthwise.

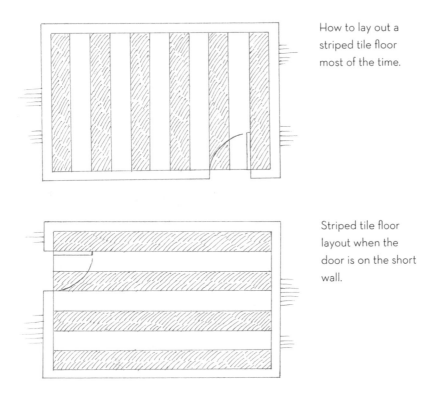

How to lay out a striped tile floor most of the time.

Striped tile floor layout when the door is on the short wall.

Basement Design Dilemma: Ho-hum Walls

- Basement walls should be interesting but not busy. The easiest way to go is putting a coat of paint on them and trimming them out with 3½- to 5-inch-wide baseboards at the floor and appropriate casing around the doors. The casings should be somewhat narrower than the base trim— 3- to 4-inch casing with 3½- to 5-inch baseboards. The smaller the room, the more slender the door trims.

- In a completely or relatively windowless room without a vibrant floor, create visual warmth and interest with a dynamically colored or patterned wall. Nine-inch-wide painted stripes are fabulous on the walls. Consider a tone on tone stripe using colors just two shades apart in the color fan book for a subtle, striking treatment.

- Paint the walls and trim the same color to visually unify an irregularly shaped and/or low-ceilinged basement. Choose a latex matte or eggshell finish paint for your walls and always satin oil or satin latex for the trim.

- To hide imperfections and add texture to the walls, clad them in wainscoting, approximately 36 to 40 inches tall. (Okay, 40 inches is pushing it, but if you really need to mask a flaw, then knock yourself out.) Be sure you've eliminated any moisture problems before installing wainscoting or it will warp. And, darling, I want you to install *wainscoting*, not *waste-coating*.

- Wallpaper is another option. Vinyl wallpaper is genius for heavily trafficked areas, especially those subject to atmospheric moisture. I love embossed wallpapers that are paintable (it's technically called *anaglypta*) or my very personal favorite, vinyl grass cloth, which replicates the stylish look of natural grass cloth but is much less fragile (= child friendly!) and is super-easy to clean.

- If your basement contains a long hallway, consider installing a chair rail along it, 36 inches from the floor to the top of the rail, and wallpapering, painting, or paneling above or below it.

Basement Design Dilemma: Low Ceilings

Paint can play heightening tricks. Avoid painting the ceiling bright white; the contrast is too sharp for a low-ceilinged space, so you'll want a warmer ivory, instead. Add a bit of the wall paint to the ceiling color (*always* test the mix first to make sure your color is right) to help elongate the walls. Most basement ceilings are too low to handle decorative touches such as crown molding. As an alternative, on an uncluttered ceiling (i.e., no pipes showing), running a 1½- to 2½-inch strip of lattice or thin base molding around the perimeter of the ceiling (not the walls) will impart visual detail and interest without eating up any vertical space, and will help make the ceiling look higher. It's hard for even a dwarf not to feel like a jolly green giant in most basements. If your ceilings are so low that you can't comfortably stand up in your basement, then relegate it to the little people in your life and designate it as Play Space Central for your children. Deemphasize looming low ceilings by drawing your eyes instead to the floor, via fascinating and eye-catching floor candy so mesmerizingly intriguing that no one will ever take their eyes off to actually bother to look up.

If you're not on a budget, consider "building" down. In urban areas, digging out the basement is an increasingly popular method for gaining ceiling height below ground. Here's the dirt: You excavate as many feet down as necessary to get the ceiling height you want. It's a pricey and complicated proposition, so definitely enlist the expertise of an architect and a contractor for this one. At the end of the day, it will pay you back in pure convenience and pleasure, not to mention resale value.

Basement Design Dilemma: Ugly, Exposed Pipes

Painting exposed ceiling pipes the same color as the ceiling helps them fade into it. Run any visible wires on top of the pipes, tying them down with plastic ties, and paint those, too.

Basement Design Dilemma: Treacherous Stairs

If you live in an older home, chances are your basement stairs are narrow enough to make a toddler feel like a linebacker. So enlarging them should be your first order of business in your below-ground design plan. Widen them as much as possible, if you can, which may well mean actually replacing them, and, while you're at it, eliminate their Alpine steepness by putting a break or turn in them if space suffices. Add an attractive handrail (not just a boring 2 by 4), and *voila!* Going down to the basement doesn't feel like you're descending to a dungeon anymore.

Cover your stairs for both style, safety (no slips!), *and* soundproofing (do I need to tell you how loud it is when your kids take a staircase at full gallop?) with an attractive, brightly patterned and durable carpet or runner. Cover plywood stairs completely; choose a runner to show a glimmer of something prettier underneath, leaving between 3 to 5 inches of stair tread exposed on either side.

Basement Design Dilemma: No Light

If structurally possible (and, um, affordable), install larger windows throughout your basement, even if they're only clerestory (small windows close to the ceiling) style. Consider rimming the perimeter of the exposed foundation with them—as many as you possibly can—to create wall-to-wall "sky" lights or a continuous transom effect.

You can trim clerestory windows or leave them untrimmed, depending on their placement. If they're awkwardly located and you'd like them to disappear, leave them trimless. To emphasize them and highlight their architectural detail, add the trim. The trick is to be consistent. If you're transforming your space into a luxurious billiard room, give it the same attention to detail and style TLC that you would if it were on the parlor floor upstairs. If you're using it as the ultimate Zen yoga studio, minimal bells and whistles will make it easier to focus on your *asanas*.

Basement Design Dilemma: Awkward Columns

Darling, here's another trick I love to both add light and to disguise unsightly basement columns: Box in weight-bearing columns with Sheetrock and electrify them to accommodate sconces. Don't be afraid to clad skinny supports simply to make them prettier and more proportionate to the room. Beef up a slender column by enclosing it in a 10- to 12-inch-wide box. Trim the crown and baseboard with molding; add panel molding or a simple $\frac{1}{2}$- to $1\frac{3}{8}$-inch-wide strip of lattice (whichever width looks best for your new column's size) nailed all around the perimeter to each facet to really gild your lily! (Search "column wraps" online for more inspiration and even prefabricated—but pricier—ones.) Electrify your columns (more on that later on) with an outlet for vacuuming and whatnot.

Or paint your newly boxed-out columns with chalkboard paint and finally let your kids write on the "walls." P.S.: Chalkboard paint below the chair rail all around is a great idea, too.

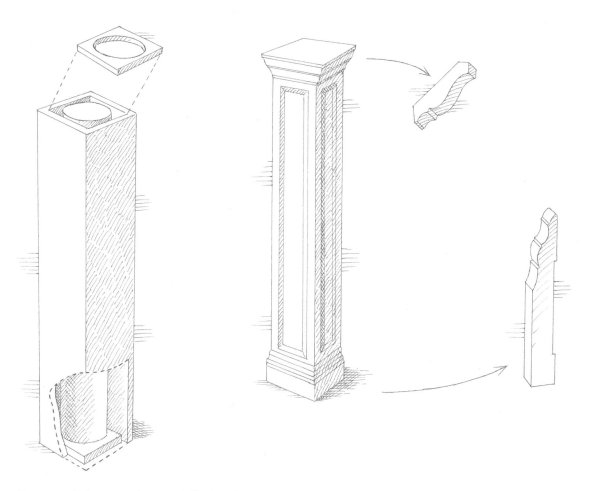

Box in weight-bearing columns with Sheetrock.

Basement Design Dilemma: Temperature and Climate Control

Proper heating and cooling is critical in a finished basement. You want to avoid its feeling like Siberia in the winter and the equator in July. Make the basement part of your household heating and cooling system, or install one that is dedicated exclusively to it.

If you live in Arctic climates (i.e., the Northeast or the Snow Belt), consider installing radiant heating under your floor or behind walls or the ceiling. Radiant heating is perfect for installation above concrete slabs, which is generally what most basement floors are made from. It's more efficient than baseboard heating and, darling, *much* better looking, to boot!

When Sheetrocking for new walls, use the thickest board your contractor recommends. Insulating between the walls will also help to keep your space dry and temperate.

Basement Design Dilemma: Ugly Door

You wouldn't put cheesy doors on the first floor of your house, so don't succumb to the temptation to hang them in the basement. Okay, downgrading your door hardware is okay, but even *that* still needs to be cute (just not as pricey)!

LIGHTING THE WAY

Basements are by definition dark and gloomy. But if you use natural and artificial light strategically, your basement can become a warm, inviting place to be. In the last section we talked about adding windows to bring in light if possible. But if that's not possible or if there still isn't enough natural light to get a subterranean glow, fake it by maxing out the artificial options. Yes, honey, you're going to have to *resort to trickery*!

Basement ceilings are typically lower than those in the rest of the house, which can make overhead lighting a challenge, and chandeliers and pendants forbidden. If you have enough room between your ceiling and the floor above—at least 6 to 9 inches—recessed lights are ideal in basements.

The 3-inch-diameter lights are cute as a button; the 6-inch ones are *not* and should be *avoided like the plague*.

(Attractive) surface-mount fixtures are another overhead lighting option.

But one *amazing* option is a fake skylight. Fake skylights, technically called *tube skylights*, are ingenious lighting devices that capture sunlight on the roof and direct it down a reflective tube into interior spaces. The tube runs through an existing chase or crawl space; one tube can light up to 500 square feet. These are easily installed in newer homes, but don't despair if your home is older—investigate the areas around your plumbing pipe stacks to see if you can squeeze something in. P.S.: Don't try this at home! Installing tube skylights requires calling in the pros.

If you're lucky enough to have a basement with a standard-height ceiling, then you can approach the overhead lighting

TRADE SECRET

Recessed lights are called high hats in the North and can lights down in Dixie. Just so we're all on the same page, sugar. ✱

as you would any other room in the house. If this is you, lucky dog, none of these rules apply (and you should definitely hang a chandelier or two down there just to make us jealous). In large spaces, installing more than one surface-mounted light fixture in a room will give you better-balanced light. Try one every 10 feet if you'll be using them as primary lighting, on more than one switch if possible. But if your room is a den, office, or lounge, get your lamp game on, because you need those soft pools of light down there, too. (Children's play spaces, on the other hand, should always be well lit from the ceiling.)

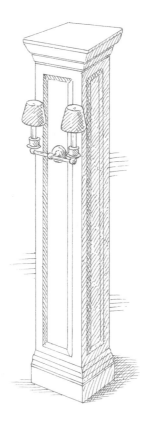

Add wall sconces to electrified boxed-in columns. Note paneled trim.

If you've boxed in your columns, they're perfect candidates for wall sconces. Put them on at least two of the four sides, wherever you need to throw a little light—or on all four if the column is in the middle of the room.

DESIGN DETAILS

Stymied about what you should dedicate your renovated basement palace to? Here are some room suggestions to get you thinking: game room, family room, TV room, home theater, office, library, kitchen, wine cellar, playroom, boom-boom room (*bachelors only!*), man cave (*a must for the happily married hus-*

band!), cigar lounge (*if you insist on smoking because you know better!*), or teenagers' lounge. Whatever it becomes, don't let it ever become a dumping ground once you've claimed it. Never confuse your fabulous new finished-and-furnished basement with mini-storage or a thrift shop. That said, the same design rules that govern the rest of your house still rule here, too . . . although you can interpret them a bit more casually below-ground.

Don't think of your basement as a depository for the decrepit! Rid it of any furniture that's broken, overly worn, or no longer works with your your new, stylish design aesthetic.

Unless you're in your charming "starter house" and know you won't be there for so long, design your souped-up basement with longevity in mind. What will it morph into after the children don't need a playroom anymore? The only thing you'll want to change to make it your home office will be paint and maybe light fixtures (something more grown-up and chicer). Plan for everything else (sufficient electrical outlets, telephone, fax, and cable lines, etc.) now.

First, *do* pay attention to your basement's entrance. It should be attractive and warmly lit. What's the first thing you see from the top of the stairs? From the landing? When you enter the room? Station a narrow console table across from the base of the stairs with a mirror (it increases the light, artificial or otherwise!) or a painting on the wall above it, with a pair of lamps on top, just as you would in an upstairs hallway. Modernists can lean an oversize floor mirror against the wall and flank it with a pair of streamlined floor lamps (stand just one in the corner if the wall isn't long enough).

Here are some tips for hanging art and adding accents in the rest of the room:

- Boxed-in columns are great spots to hang art. Consider stacking several pieces vertically for impact, especially if the columns are among the first things you see when you walk in. Try not to have your art exceed the column's width, although ignore this rule if you're hanging your Picasso.
- Sheets of mirrors affixed to the wall from floor to ceiling visually expand the space and are especially great if you're using the space as a gym (the better to watch your waist shrink as you work out!). If you're not a fan of the floor-to-ceiling mirrored effect, try large framed mirrors or a collection of smaller ones, either hung on the wall or propped up against it. And mirroring the interior of recessed clerestory windows is nothing short of brilliant.

TRADE SECRET   Using great expanses of sheet mirror to visually enlarge a space and increase reflected light is one of decorators' oldest tricks in the book.

- Dress up long, seemingly endless lengths of furniture-less wall with oversize pieces of framed art, like vintage travel posters and amateur paintings.

- Select an entire basement wall or hallway for a floor-to-ceiling collage of framed family photos. Stack them cheek by jowl, horizontally and vertically. Unify your frames by choosing a single color (i.e., black, gold, silver, white, maple) or frame style.

- Don't forget the faux fireplace. Whether you go for a super-opulent, built-in, could-that-be-real one, or more of a straight-out-of-the-box, plug-n-play, cheap-and-cheery number, faux fireplaces make awesome focal points in architecturally challenged, below-ground spaces. *J'adore!* ✱

LAUNDRY ROOMS

9

They were once the gulags of the home, veritable slave quarters for the mistress of the house, banished to the least accessible, most forlorn corner of the home. Who *wouldn't* get depressed doing laundry? Today, your washer and dryer's space commands the same kind of consideration you give your kitchen and dining room. It *is* essential that the space be functional, full of clever storage, and comfortable—but you want it to look good, too! Like a powder room, the laundry can handle over-the-top themed décor—the bolder the better. Now, themes are unquestionably tacky anywhere else in the house, but the laundry room gets a *free pass.* Indulge in your most shameful design peccadilloes, including the embarrassing ones, like your secret Mets obsession. Think of it this way: It's a pretty safe bet that you'll be the only person to ever set foot in your laundry lounge. Guests may sneak into your private bathroom, but your laundry room? Not a chance. So go ahead and indulge your cheetah-print fetish and cover every surface in there with it. Honey, I wouldn't say no to faux-finishing the washer and dryer with an animal print, too! On the other hand, appliance manufacturers have helped the cause along by turning out machines in enough shades and styles to match every shoe in your closet. Best of all, these newfangled washers and dryers practically load themselves. (Now, if they could only sort darks from whites!) While waiting for that feature, focus on all the groovy accessories out there just begging to be used to trick out your space.

THE LAYOUT

It's *your* laundry room, so set it up to accommodate not only your every laundry need but also your every laundry desire. Like real estate, the most appealing laundry rooms are a function of their location . . . location, location. Easy access—to the space and the washer and dryer—is key.

If you're in a position to pick a location for your laundry room, the ideal spot is near the bedroom or at the very least near or in the bathroom, where a water supply and ventilation presumably exists.

If your laundry room is currently in the basement, consider installing an additional stackable washer/dryer unit in a closet or other unused space near your bedroom. Remember, there's no reason that anyone living in the twenty-first century should have to haul a load of laundry down the stairs just because servants used to. Since we're our own servants now, it's time for the washer and dryer to come to us! Save the larger side-by-side unit in the basement for bigger loads and bulkier items.

If you are lucky enough to have a room dedicated to doing laundry (alas, city dwellers, one day . . . one day—see tips for you in the next section), kit it out to make the space a pleasant place to be in and the job as pleasurable as possible. Lay it out so you can gracefully glide from one task to the next without a trace of frustration. You've got a *whole room*—max out every square inch. Set up an ironing station, a sorting

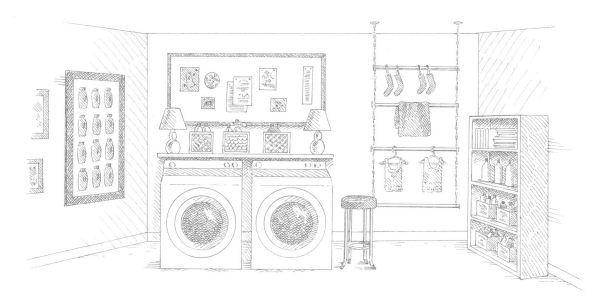

Make your laundry room a laundry *oasis*.

and folding area, and a hand-washing space. Set up a coat rack or great set of hooks for air-drying here (and not on your shower curtain rod, even though it's tempting).

Creating a Laundry "Space" with No Laundry Room

If you don't have a room that you can dedicate, the good news is that today's ventless dryers can turn almost any closet into an instant laundry room. If you live in the land of the unvented (i.e., an apartment), you can convert any dryer to a ventless model by investing in an attachable condensation vent, which collects the moisture from your dryer into a small cup that you empty periodically. However, they still emit enough moisture in the air that it's a better bet to go with the true ventless models, which are also typically magnificently apartment sized.

In terms of layout, in a hallway closet you can position the washer and dryer side by side, then build in shelves or cabinets above them to hold supplies. Install a Murphy-bed-style ironing board, which you can neatly tuck away inside the closet, on a door or wall when not in use.

If you have room in the bathroom or kitchen, those are both great places for a laundry space. A stackable washer and dryer is ideal in this situation. Some stackables feature a pull-out shelf between the two appliances for folding items straight from the dryer. Pair them with a shelving unit that can accommodate several baskets for laundry and accoutrements.

If your stackables are in the kitchen, hide them behind a tall pantry-style door that matches your cabinetry. If you can't tuck them behind one vertical door, then stack two smaller doors on top of each other to get the effect.

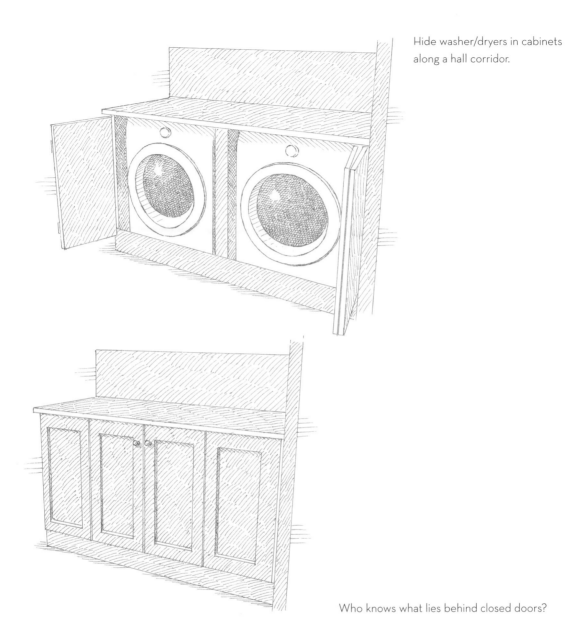

Hide washer/dryers in cabinets along a hall corridor.

Who knows what lies behind closed doors?

The best thing about locating the laundry in your loo, if there's room, is its marvelous proximity to where your clothes both pile up (we refer to your bedroom chair!) and are put away (in your closet and chest of drawers). And your bathroom floors and finishes are already humidity proof, too. (Although you may still want to sit the washer in a pan, just in case.)

SIZE MATTERS

Here's the scoop on the numbers you need to know:

- Although sizes still vary, most washers and dryers are about 37 inches wide and 27 to 32 inches deep. Stackable units are 24 to 27 inches wide and about 24 inches deep.
- When selecting a new unit, compare the cubic feet each unit can contain to determine which holds the most laundry.
- You'll need a minimum of 36 inches in front of the washer and dryer for ease of movement; if the washer and dryer are tucked into a closet along a corridor or positioned opposite each other, leave at least 4 feet of space in front of them so that others can pass by as you do the laundry.
- Overall dimensions of work areas will vary depending on the washer and dryer dimensions, but for standard appliances, the amount of floor area needed for a stacked washer/dryer = 43 by 63 inches; straight line arrangement = 62 by 66 inches.
- If you're putting shelves behind your top-loading washing machine, make sure they are positioned so that that the top, when open, clears the shelves.
- Give yourself at least 3 feet of cleared space to fold clothes. For small spaces, use a hinged drop-down shelf for tuck-it-away storage.

- Leave at least 3 feet around the perimeter of an ironing board (in its upright position) for ease of navigating.

THE COVER-UP: STYLE AND EFFECT

I can't say it enough: Laundry rooms are like powder rooms in that they are typically on the small side. Unlike powder rooms, though, it's virtually guaranteed that no one who is not related to you will ever see yours, so be encouraged to *truly* go for broke in making your laundry lounge a splendiferous treat for your eyes only—it's the one room where no theme is too kitschy and no style out of bounds.

If you're a bachelor, go for the camouflage look. If you love the tropics, work that tropical fish theme. A color scheme of regency red with black trim is elegant in that English country way, as is oodles of chintz and toile de Jouy.

But before you decide to turn your laundry room into an exact replica of animal print paradise at Graceland, think through practical needs first: Surfaces should be easy to clean, and storage should be as easily accessible as it is stylish.

Trick out the walls of your laundry room just as you would any other room—paint them a vibrant color like lipstick red (a fab contrast to white appliances) in an easy-to-clean washable matte latex finish, or wallpaper them in extravagant yet washable wallpaper (as diminutive as most laundries are, splurging on pricey paper is an affordable proposition!).

Leaving a plain concrete floor in your laundry room is a design no-no. The floor *must* be finished. As a general rule, any flooring that works in the basement will work here. Although remember, your washer just might overflow one day.

Install a great indoor/outdoor area rug, laminate flooring, or gorgeous ceramic or vinyl tile. If you're installing a new floor, consider laying out tile (ceramic, vinyl, or indoor/outdoor) in a pattern. Concentric geometrical figures (i.e., square in square, circle in circle) look great. If you're stuck with a concrete floor, paint it using marine deck paint or have it epoxied in a bright color by a professional, both using water-resistant materials. At the very least, lay down a brightly colored area rug.

Furnish the laundry room. If you've abandoned your TV room armoire now that you've splurged on the fancy flat screen, retrofit the shelves to suit your laundry room storage needs. If it doesn't go with your themed décor, paint or stain it to match. Place a couple of small-scale dining room chairs or decorative stools in your laundry room either just for visual appeal or to perch or for your laundry-day chat fest with a friend.

Function and Form

One reason people *hate* to do laundry is because they are not well organized or they have an uncomfortable setup for the task! Consider these simple rules and tips:

- Think about how you use your laundry room and arrange supplies accordingly. Detergents should be within easy reach; your emergency stain supplies, attractively corralled in a basket or large jar, can be stashed on a high shelf.

- Mount a bath-towel rod on the underside of a shelf to hang shirts on hangers. If that's not an option, install a tension rod in the doorway so that you can hang clothes as they come out of the dryer. It means less ironing, so . . .

- Install decorative hooks at least one hanger's width apart for drip-drying or hang a rod from a handsome chain secured into the ceiling with anchors along the length or width of the room to do the same job.

- Have fun with physics and figure out how heavy a rack full of wet clothes actually is, then make sure you secure the chain accordingly. Remind your children and pets that it's not a trapeze.

- Install rows of hooks along a wall also for drip-drying in high style. If you have bulky materials, though, consider protecting the wall behind them with either large sheets of acrylic screwed in the wall (get them at art supply stores—photographers use them during photo shoots) or vinyl wallpaper or rubber padding tacked to the wall.

- Outfit the room with everything you need to do hand laundry: expandable drying racks, a retractable clothesline (you'll wonder how you ever got along without one), a deep, oversize utility sink, racks galore, and clothespins, which come in so many cute colors these days! Minimalists, use binder clips from the home office department, and those of you going for the Zen vibe, stick to the classic wooden variety.

- Install a peg rack behind the washer to hang stray socks, keys, and other pocketed items that don't belong in the washer.

- If ironing is a meditative exercise for you, make sure you are standing on a padded area rug or rubber mat so you can iron for as long as it takes to clear your mind (and save your back!).

Arrange multiple hooks to create a stylish drying wall.

LIGHTING

Make sure your laundry room is as beautifully lit as your kitchen is. That is, include ambient, decorative, and task lighting in the scheme so the room feels less like a workspace and more like a real room that you really want to be in. Indulge your desire to hang *whatever* you want overhead. If a chandelier invokes *ooohs* and *aaahs*—even just from you—then go for it. Anything goes, the quirkier the better. As much as the experts will tell you that a brightly lit laundry room is the path to clean clothes perfection, darling, I beg to differ. Yes, recessed task lights are helpful when you're mating socks, but do you really want to toil under the glare of harsh overhead lights? The truth is that bathing the room in lamplight gives it a lovely warm glow that makes sudsing up a far more elegant affair, which is why I recommend stationing a lamp on either side of the washer and dryer or placing a tiny pair on a shelf. Turn the overhead task lighting on only under duress (unless, of course, it's that cute chandelier)!

Incandescent bulbs are the typical choice for bright task lighting, and truthfully, your Designer Girlfriend here actually prefers them for lighting most living spaces in a house (the Green Team is going to murder me!). The laundry room is one of the few zones in your home for which I recommend compact fluorescents, which, although they do use less energy, create less heat, and last up to ten times longer than standard incandescents, they also emit the most unflattering light ever. When you can, opt for warm fluorescent bulbs, which are (marginally but we'll take it) more flattering than the cool ones.

Sconces are the wall bling of a laundry room. Hang them in a symmetrical fashion if they're on more than one wall—whatever happens on one wall should also happen at the same location on the other, because a sconce in the middle of one wall and in the corner of the other causes visual vertigo, which is definitely a design don't.

DESIGN DETAILS

Art

Give yourself something other than utilitarian items to look at on your laundry room walls! Fill them with art, laundry-themed or otherwise. If you didn't already hang those four thousand family photos along a hallway or staircase, cover the walls of your laundry room with them.

Giant pinboards add panache to your laundry space. Create your own by mounting large stick-on corkboard tiles or several small ones in geometric shapes or evenly spaced along one wall. Painted or fabric-covered squares of cork or thick foamcore (use spray adhesive to affix cloth to the front and packing or duct tape to attach it to the back) also are genius for pinning up images galore. Sugar, when you simply refuse to let your laundry room be the dreariest room in the house, wash day immediately becomes a whole lot more fun!

Design Tip

For those of you who can't be without your media, what better place to indulge your private passion for dubious television shows than in the laundry room? No reality show is too tawdry to watch if you're pressing linens at the same time! If music makes the job go faster, install an iPod docking station or old-school boom box on a shelf and do your best karaoke while you work.

Chic Storage

Storage is key and should be cute. Don't limit your storage shopping to the closet/storage department, though; stroll the home office, bath, and kitchen aisles for clever options. I love the storage cubes in the home office section for laundry room elegance: Buy them in bulk and stack against a wall for a great geometric look. Chic bookcases are perfect for holding laundry baskets and other large bins for storing bulk items. Canvas tote bags also make attractive—and washable—containers, too.

Store cleansers and detergents in similar containers. If you're going for the gold medal in utilitarian chic, decant detergent and bleach from their ho-hum packaging into clear glass containers with stylish hand- or computer-made labels.

Elegantly store laundry essentials in a styled-up bookcase.

Not only does this look smart (think of a display at Tiffany's!), but you can also see the contents. If you are big box store devotee (and always have extra detergent on hand), go for the graphic beauty of repetition and line up multiples. Channel your inner Warhol and turn those improbably huge containers into sculpture. (By the way, *anything* becomes a piece of sculpture when you display lots of it!)

If storage is open to view, approach it like a visual merchandiser might at your favorite department store. Style your shelves, don't just merely fill them! Lay them out like you would your Christmastime mantel, and now we're cooking with gas! To cover open storage that simply can't be made attractive (or if you are too resolute a slob to do anything about it, which we all are sometimes, honey), mount a canvas shade or hang a curtain over the shelves to gracefully hide supplies.

WINDOW TREATMENTS

10

Windows are the soul of your house, and your window treatments are the eyes of that soul. *Especially* at night, when bare windows seem more like black holes, no matter *how* fabulous the view is during the day. Whether tailored, crisp, and minimalist or lavishly over the top, dressed windows finish a room. So if you're staring at your neighbor's garage through unadorned glass as you read this, sugar, you're not done decorating! (*Note*: If you have floor-to-ceiling glass walls in your stunning modernist home and no nosy neighbors within miles, then we'll give you a hall pass on this one, dollface, but I want you to take the millions—*just kidding!*—you'll save going curtainless and invest that money in breathtaking outdoor lighting so there's something brilliantly lit to look at through your windows twenty-four hours a day.)

Like most decorative exercises, window dressing is equal parts style and function. They need to control excessive light from the outside and also give you privacy from the prying eyes of passersby checking out your stylish interiors. They should prevent a room from turning into a sauna in the summer and an igloo in the winter. And nothing can be better at decorative sleight of hand than cleverly sized and creatively mounted curtains, blinds, or shades to beautify, camouflage, or coordinate oddly shaped, located, or detailed windows.

After your walls, windows take up the most visible visual real estate in your home—think about it, darling: furniture and area rugs cover most of the floor—so I want to encourage you to not make window treatments an *afterthought* in your design plan, and I don't want you to stint on them, either (save stinting for the bathroom!). Even if you don't actually *execute* them till the very, very end of decorating your home, take what you'll be putting at your windows into consideration from the moment you lay eyes on your them—that way it'll be easier for you to start imagining the finished room in your head.

Here's a little tutorial on window types to get us started:

Window Types

Most windows are framed in wood, steel, or aluminum. *Sash windows* consist of two framed parts ("sashes") that hold glass and slide either up and down or side to side. The vertically sliding numbers, one on top of the other, are called *double-hung sash windows*, or *double-hung windows* for short. These are the most common ones you see, as opposed to *horizontal sliding sash windows*, also known as *gliders*. *Casement windows* feature a pair of windows that swing open, either inward or outward, like French doors, sometimes (but not always) with a crank. (*Extra credit*: If you're going for chateau chic, have your casement windows hinged, like they are in Europe.) *Tilt and turn* windows are newfangled creations that either tilt inward at the top or open wide via a side hinge (and boy, can these babies be hard to operate!). *Tilt and slide windows* tilt inward at the top; one part of the window can slide horizontally open, too. *Awing* or *projected windows* are hinged at the bottom or the top to either prop or drop open. If you live in Florida, you might have *jalousie windows*, with many slits of glass that open like a Venetian blind, using a crank. *Bay* or *bow windows* feature at least three window panels set at different angles (bay) or a curve (bow). *Palladian windows* have adorable arched tops; fancy ones have smaller side windows called *sidelights*. If you have a regular window with a separate little arched window above, the upper arched thingee is called a *fanlight*. *Picture windows* are large, single-paned windows that frame a stunning view; they are *fixed windows*, since they don't open. *Whew! Are you seeing the light yet???*

On we go! The larger pieces of wood or metal that frame the big halves of the window (i.e., upper/lower or left/right) are called *mullions*. The smaller pieces of wood that divide each sash into smaller segments like a grille are called *muntins*; the little-bitty panes of glass that the muntins divide a window into are called *lights*. Still with me? When you have more than one "light," you've got a *divided light window*! *Simulated* or *snap-on*

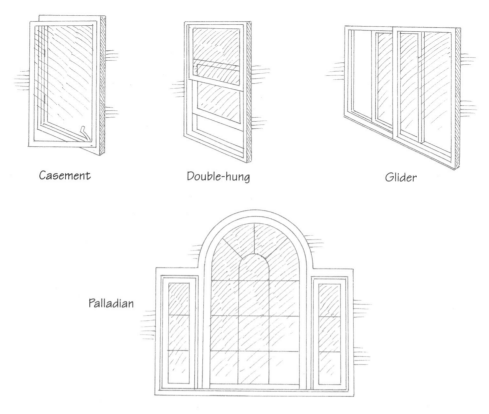

Casement

Double-hung

Glider

Palladian

Basic types of windows.

divided lights (one piece of glass per sash with faux muntins made of a single piece of wood or whatnot screwed or snapped on top) can fake the look of *true divided lights* (each "light" is made from a separate piece of glass, the old-fashioned way) for less. *And last but not least!* Divided-light windows are often identified by the number of lights each sash is divided into: *one over one, nine over six, six over six, four over four,* or by a look that's typical of an era (i.e., *Prairie-style, Victorian-style*). It's always a nice idea to match your window style to your home's exterior style and/or period (whether real or faking it marvelously, darling). *Class dismissed!*

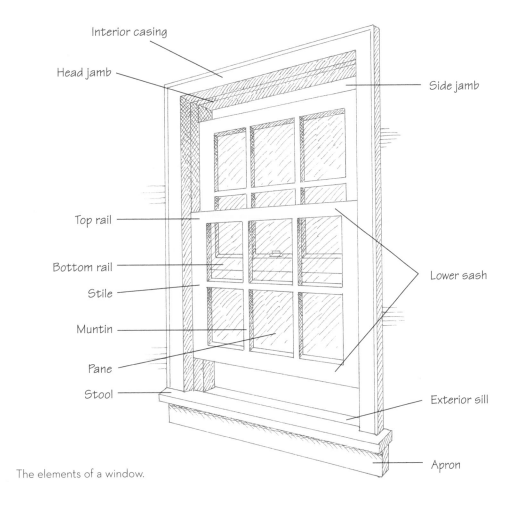

Interior casing

Head jamb

Side jamb

Top rail

Bottom rail

Stile

Muntin

Pane

Stool

Lower sash

Exterior sill

Apron

The elements of a window.

WINDOW TREATMENTS

A great American decorator once said that the term *window treatments* sounded like a medical procedure, but, honey, it *sure is practical*! And the term conveys the thought perfectly, too, so let's play doctor! The nattily dressed window should almost always have a two-part window treatment: (A) Something very close to the window (frequently, but not always, inside the window recess—BTW, pros refer to the zone inside the recess that holds the window as the "window box") to control light and give privacy, i.e., a blind, shade, or shutter, and (B) Something more decorative that enhances the room's décor on the wall outside the window frame, like curtains. *Window Treatment News Flash!* Unless you have curtains on a traverse rod (like the ones in hotels that open and close by pulling on a cord at the side), it's less wear-and-tear on your (fabulous, pricey) curtains (did I mention *pricey*?) to just leave them stationary all the time and let your blinds or shades do the heavy lifting of daily opening and closing and adjusting for light and privacy. With a blind or shutter, you'll always be able to see outside (and you can adjust how much!), unless you close them completely; fabric or textured shades offer more decorative chutzpah but will leave you, um, *exposed* when you raise them completely or at half-mast to let the light enter during the day.

Blinds and Shutters

Slatted *blinds* and louvered *shutters* are the most streamlined and versatile window treatments out there. They're great for controlling light (you can adjust them throughout the day as the sun beats down on your dwelling), privacy (tilting the slats with the edge closest to you going up allows you to see out while outsiders can't see in; doing the reverse allows more light in but less privacy), and discreetly blocking a bad view (tilt the slats just enough to prevent a clear view of that brick wall you face and you're golden!). Blinds or shutters mounted *inside* the window frame's recess are called *inside mount*; those mounted *outside* the window frame's recess, *beyond* the window's trim (if there *is* trim) are called *outside mount* (surprise!).

I love blinds or shutters alone for a crisp, minimalist look in both modern and traditional rooms and am crazy about them hung inside the box, an inch in front of the window itself, beneath curtains for a layered window treatment that also works in any style of space (see more, below).

Venetian Blinds

Aluminum Venetian ("slatted") blinds were S.O.P. in the 1930s and '40s, and *boy, were they frumpy*! I'm pleased to report

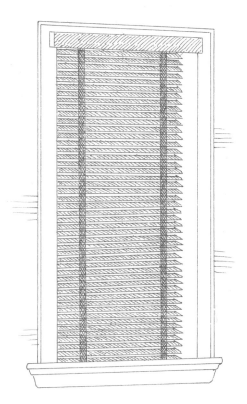

Wood Venetian blinds with cloth tape ladders.

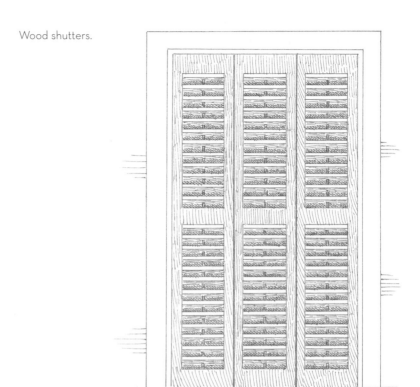

Wood shutters.

that the blind industry has been busy as bees in the style department since the war, though, and if you haven't thought
about Venetian blinds in a while, it's time to think again!
They! Look! Gorgeous!

Today's blinds come in tons of materials (wood, *exotic* wood,
waterproof faux wood for wet spaces, aluminum, fabric sheers
that mimic the slatted blind effect) and sizes from $5/8$-inch-
wide minis to $2 5/8$-inch jumbos and up. Two-inch slats and
up are best for residential settings (P.S.: the wider the slat,
the more daylight the blind lets in); nothing screams "meet

you in the conference room at three" louder than mini-blinds, so unless you just *have* to have them (in which case, honey, we do understand), leave the slender slats at the office.

Wood slat blinds were traditionally made from basswood, lightweight, easily stained, and (especially) warp resistant. Loads of other species are used today, but basswood still rules. Aluminum blinds can be more contemporary-looking and also come in ten thousand different colors (I exaggerate only slightly), which is a plus when trying to match your blind color to your walls' paint color (*very* chic, dahling). It's hard to find wood blinds in widths over 96 inches, but aluminum blinds can come up to 196 inches wide, which is *mah-ve-lous* for very wide windows or covering multiple windows with one large blind, no matter what style of décor.

Design Tip

If you're going for stained wood blinds, take your hardwood floor as a starting point, colorwise. Blinds almost always look best when closely matched to the room's floor color. If you have lots of beefy, gleaming white trim, though (and especially for bedrooms and baths), matching your blinds to the trim color can look great, too.

I love the decorative *cloth* (or *twill*) tape *ladders* that are attached to Venetian blinds (they're the little vertical strips of webbing that run the length of the blind on both sides). They help hold the slats together and camouflage the operating string running through the center of the slats. I'll confess that I am *maniacal* about having cloth tape ladders on both wood and aluminum slat blinds—they're gorgeous and a blind looks plain naked without them! (Eek! A *bald blind!*) But in a rare moment of sanity, let me be practical and confide that they *do* block a bit of the incoming light and also obstruct a bit of the view outside, *just! in! case! that! matters!*

Venetian blinds operate with either cord-only (tilt on the left side, raise on the right) or cord + wand (a cord raises the blind, a plastic wand tilts the slats) operation. Your Designer Friend Here wants you to know that wands are a no-no. No. No. No, no, no. Ditto for vertical slat blinds (unless you are designing for the *Bob Newhart Show* reunion).

Whichever size, style, or finish you go for, *do* be your BBF (blinds' best friend) and *dust* those suckers every once in a while! Nothing obstructs a view more than dust!

Pleated Honeycomb Blinds

Like the beehives whose form they resemble, the cell-shaped pleats of honeycomb blinds are havens of energy efficiency. They're great options for close-to-the-window treatments that can help reduce a room's energy loss during frosty weather. Pleat sizes range from 3/8 inch to 1 inch and up, and these blinds come in both paper and fabric versions (choose fabric ones for the most energy retention, and get the best quality you can afford). Honeycomb blinds operate with a pull-cord mechanism.

Vaned Window Shadings

If you like the light- and privacy-controlling features and look of a slatted Venetian blind but prefer the soft elegance of a fabric window treatment, then you'll find vaned window shadings irresistible. They're made of thin fabric "vanes," 2 to 5 inches wide, sandwiched between layers of translucent sheers, and they work on a continuous cord tilt-and-raise mechanism (one cord does both). As you pull the cord, the

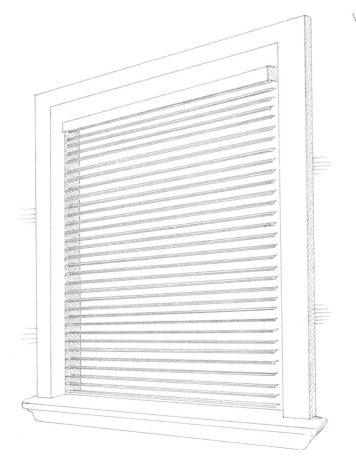

Vaned window shade.

vanes open, tilt, and close, just like true slatted blinds, and then the entire shade can be raised to disappear in its headrail.

Matchstick or Bamboo Blinds

Okay, so they're technically shades and not blinds (because they roll up with a cord like a blind), but with this much style at this low a price, *who's asking*!!! As inexpensive as they are chic, matchstick blinds are made of toothpick-thin slats of wood loosely threaded together and stained or left natural. Originating in Asia, these blinds were once almost exclusively in tortoiseshell bamboo but now come in gobs of great-looking materials and finishes. Depending on their density and the opacity of the material used to back them, matchstick blinds can allow either a little, a lot, or no light to penetrate them.

They're perfect for layered window treatments when you're looking for a natural option that delivers more texture, style, and visual drama than a plain wood blind. And talk about versatile! Matchstick blinds might be the only window treatment that you'll find as often on Park Avenue as you will in dorm rooms everywhere—democratic chic! *J'adore!*

Roller Shades

These are the T. rex of the window-covering industry—*you know* roller shades probably were in an early cave dwelling and will be showing up at the Smithsonian any day now!!!! These simple, spring-rolled cloth or paper window treatments come in dozens of styles and even more colors. You can choose from those that pull down from the top, up from

Tortoiseshell matchstick blinds look elegant beneath curtains.

the bottom, or do both, in transparencies that run the gamut from Madonna's-hotel-room-can't-see-my-hand-in-front-of-me-midnight-is-my-only-time-of-day black-out shades to semi-opaque to sheer-and-clear translucent. They can be trimmed at the bottom edge with braid, fringe, or beading or bordered with ribbon along their two sides and lower edge. Sugar, the possibilities are *endless!* Take a ho-hum store-bought shade from zero to sixty stylewise in a matter of minutes by covering it with your own fabulous fabric or wall-paper (search online for detailed instructions).

Roller blinds and shades are perfectly handsome on their own—and *geeeenius* for you Relentlessly Modern Minimalists—or stylishly layered beneath curtains.

Roman Shades

Roman shades, tailored panels of fabric that pull up into broad, flat pleats via cords tied to tiny loops on their reverse sides, are the little black dresses of window treatments. Depending on their cut, installation (inside or outside mount), and material (boldly patterned fabric or plain cotton duck?), Roman shades can be monastically simple, extravagantly over the top, and anything in between; these darlings look fabulous just about anywhere. Speaking of fabulosity, the *best* Roman shades are always lined (unless you are going for the sheer shade effect, in which case, honey, just ignore me)—they pleat more neatly when raised and have a more elegant visual heft when lowered. (While we're at it: Layering a sheer Roman shade, with either a straight bottom edge or one with softly raised corners at the lower edge, beneath a pair of curtains looks very twenty-first-century chic.)

Thermal Shades

There's always one know-it-all in the bunch, and these energy-saving shades get the award in the Smarty Pants Shades department. Made from plastic sheeting or special weaves, thermal shades provide sun control through tiny microlouvers. A mechanized system featuring light and/or heat sensors responds to the temperature and amount of light streaming in and raises or lowers the blinds accordingly. Any smarter and they'd be taking out the dog daily, too!

TRADE SECRET

Choosing a continuous loop, bead chain clutch operation instead of the standard spring-roller mechanism will save you endless hours of annoying blinds snapping shut and flapping about and eliminate your need to climb a ladder to get them back down again. ✳

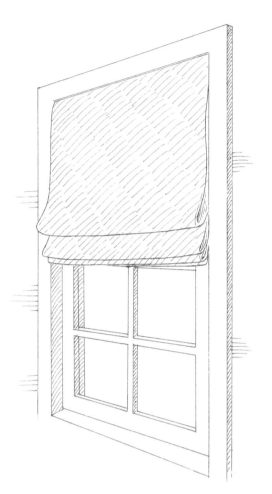

Roman shade with flat-bottomed edge.

Drapery and Curtains

Fabric draped from a rod in front of a window becomes curtains, and nothing adds more warmth and style to a finished room—even the most Zenlike spaces. (Have I said that before?) In the truest sense of the term, *draperies* are fancier curtains, floor length and more detailed in their execution, expanding *beyond* the window frame; true *curtains*, on the other hand, are hung *within* the window frame, and can be attached

Roman shade with soft-bottomed edge.

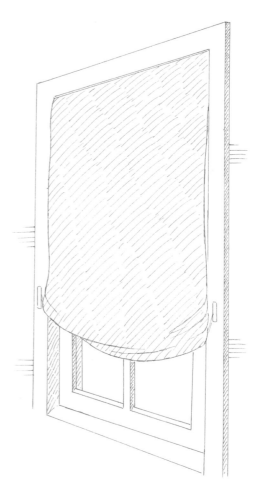

to the actual window sash itself (like those cute little café curtains that cover a window's lower half). Now that you're an expert in window treatment technology (W.T.T. to the initiated, *dahling*), know that the two terms are virtually synonymous today (although style cognoscenti *do* tend to refer to them both as *curtains*, which, I'll confess, is why I do, too).

Curtains are made by sewing together long widths of fabric (most decorative fabric is 54 inches wide), backing that with widths of fabric lining (lined curtains hang better—if you have the option, always choose lined curtains), and creatively pleating the whole shebang along the upper edge to add fullness and, um, drape (the lower edge gets hemmed). *Draw curtains*, which are what you almost always think of when curtains come to mind, consist of a set of two curtain panels that meet in the middle of the window when drawn together (see more about determining curtain panel width below). The two vertical edges that meet are called *leading edges* (*inside leading edges* to be anal about it); the outside vertical edges are called *exterior edges*. Trimming the leading edges with a decorative trim or braid ups a curtain's cute ante.

Curtains attach to the rods that hold them via hooks inserted into the heading's pleats or via other stylish options like tabs. Here are some great-looking curtain header styles:

Nothing else adds a layer of texture (and color and/or pattern) to a room like curtains, and almost every room needs them. (Am I being repetitive yet?) Skimping on curtain width is the biggest mistake design neophytes make, so here's the foolproof formula for you superstars: *As a rule, curtain width should always be at least twice the width of the window (or space they cover) for fullness.* If you're having pleated curtains custom made, the *unpleated* width of fabric will be twice the width of your window; when pleated up and hung, they will be *exactly* the width of your window . . . at the curtains' *top*. If you're using ready-made curtain panels, make sure to purchase an even number of panels that equals at least twice your window's width for fullness, and then divide them into two "pairs" on the rod. (Join edges together of combined panels using iron-on fabric seaming tape if you're not the stitching type; or better yet, ask your dry cleaner to sew them together for you, which they'll do inexpensively.)

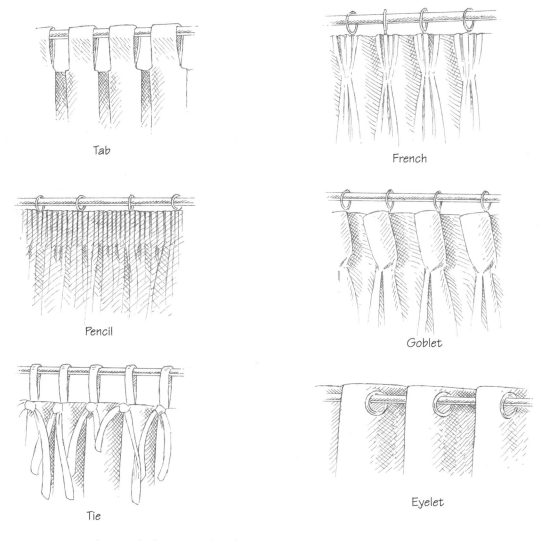

Tab

French

Pencil

Goblet

Tie

Eyelet

Six great-looking curtain headers.

For modern rooms, opt for clean-lined, simply headed (French pleats or similar) curtains of minimal fullness (just twice the window's width, or even just 1¾ times the window's width if you want *reeeeeally* sleek); the lusher and more traditional you go, up the width proportionately up to 2¾ times the window's width (although 2¾ will definitely give you a ballgown effect, Scarlett).

Hanging Curtains

Curtains should always be installed as close to the ceiling line as possible in order to visually elongate your windows and uplift your ceiling. A-L-W-A-Y-S. (Unless you live in a cha-

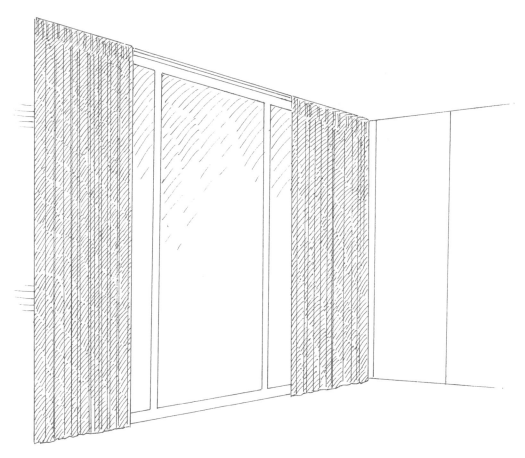

Cover the entire wall with curtains to create the effect of ginormous windows.

teau with 20-foot ceilings, of course, darling, in which case your chief of staff is probably reading this book *for* you.) Leave an inch or just over to accommodate the curtain rod's brackets and the tops of the curtain rings, but *aim high*!

The reason you see curtains hung so close to windows—and *shamelessly* installed on the *very face* of the trim, a Hall of Fame Don't if ever there *was*—in catalogs is to help vendors sell short, stubby little panels, those clever, crafty creatures. Now that you're on to their secret, though, you'll know to keep shopping until you find the longest, cutest ones for your room's ceiling height and outfox them! (Yippee!)

Never end your curtains exactly at the window trim. Extending the rod by at least 6 to 8 inches past the outer edge of the trim on *each side* of the window will let in bushels of light (what you want) when the curtains are open (you'll part them so that the leading edge *just* stops before the window glass ends and the trim starts), makes your windows look gargantuan (your eye doesn't know where the window really ends and the wall begins—it thinks the glass continues past the curtained part, and we're taking full advantage of the optical illusion!) *and* show off your lovely curtain fabric, too (since there's more of it to see!). *Talk about your multitasking tips!* If you have tiny little windows on large expanses of wall, feel free to increase the amount of wall space your curtains cover as much as you'd like in order to "create" the windows of your dreams!

THE COVER-UP: STYLE AND EFFECT

Now that you've got the basic elements of window treatments down pat, how do you put them together? Blinds? Curtains?

Both? And what on *earth* is a valence? Here's more scoop on the Curtain Call, doll:

- Consider using an *inside-mounted* blind, shutter, or shade, all by itself, without curtains, if:
  - You have windows framed with ga-ga gorgeous, beefy trim and you want to highlight that (*especially* if the room is small or low-ceilinged).
  - You have a radiator cover beneath your window that sticks out too far and don't want to alter your ceiling line above the window to accommodate floor-to-ceiling curtains.
  - You're going for Calvin Klein, super-Zen sleekness and even the simplest curtain would be too frou-frou for you.
  - You have nicely trimmed windows in a tiny room with no wall space adjacent to the windows' trim to accommodate curtains (if even one side is too small, bunny, then they all are).
- Consider using an *outside-mounted* blind, shutter, or shade, all by itself, without curtains, if:
  - You have an awkwardly shaped or located window with no trim (more on this shortly).
  - You have a small window that needs to look larger.
  - Anytime you have a trimless window and *reeeeeally* can't stand the froufiness of curtains (in spite of my incessantly urging you to think about it).
- Treat all the windows in one room with the same style of window treatment, even if the windows are an odd match, with identical curtains or blinds. If they're on different walls and *reeeeeally* differently sized, it's okay to vary the

Pop quiz! As a rule, a window should have either a _____ or a _____ closer to the window to adjust for light and privacy, and the curtains on the outside should remain _____, because they are actually used more to _____ the walls of the _____ they're in.

Extra credit! If you have floor-to-ceiling glass windows, and _____ nosy _____, then *lucky you* can _____ your windows _____! But you should be sure to _____ the landscape outside so it is _____ at night and you'll have something _____ to _____ at on the other side of the _____ twenty-four hours a _____!

treatment, but use the same fabric or material for consistency. (Like when one wall works for curtains and the other wall's Wee Willy windows call for Roman shades. P.S.: Always consider an outside-mounted Roman shade first, if appropriate, here, so you can see more of the fabric you're using and max out the homogeneity.)

- If you're blessed with either several windows in a row with very little space in between or one extra-wide window, max out its scale and drama by dressing it with one single curtain and a single shade or blind beneath. Extend the curtain's width on either side at least 8 inches to 1 foot, or more if there is empty wall space just begging to be covered.

- And while we're at it, bay windows almost always look better when treated as a single window, unless the wall space between each individual window is greater than 15 inches.

Dressing extra wide window.

- Nothing can be more vexing than attacking a window with a radiator cover below. *Resist the temptation* to end your curtains halfway down the wall just to accommodate what's sticking out below! (Honey, this looked awful at Desi and Lucy's, and it still looks horrible today!) Instead, if you're an owner, have your contractor build out a soffit at the ceiling above the window so that the new wall will protrude 2 to 3 inches *beyond* the radiator cover's front edge. The soffit will give you something to hang your curtain rod from and allow your curtains to cascade soft and flowingly,

Build a soffit at the ceiling to accommodate a radiator cover below.

unencumbered, to the ground. Install your blinds or shade in the newly created recess under the soffit (your windows will look brilliantly recessed!). If you're dressing windows in your adorable rental, go for Roman shades.

- Fake larger windows for the size-challenged fenestraters out there with these simple rules:

  ■ Combine the curtained wall technique (page 207) with an oversize Roman shade closer to the window:

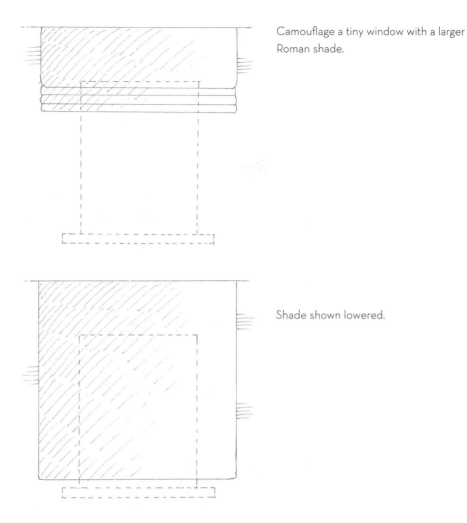

Camouflage a tiny window with a larger Roman shade.

Shade shown lowered.

Outside-mount a shade beneath the curtain so that the top of the shade hits the vertical middle of the curtain rod. The shade's uppermost line will be invisible and *poof*! Your shade will look as if it's magically floating on the walls, especially since you'll also cleverly extend its width far enough beyond the actual window frame for the shade's sides to be invisible, too. (End your shade just before the curtains end on either side.)

- Try the above tip with floor-length tailored sheers, which look great in more traditional settings.
- For more contemporary spaces, the supersize Roman shade trick works on its own *sans* curtains. Outside-mount the shade at the ceiling line and extend its sides at least 4 to 5 inches beyond the window opening or trim on each side.
- If you have a small or awkwardly located window that you'd like to better blend with the walls (and not stand out as glorious), outside-mount a plain Roman shade made in *solid-colored fabric* that matches the wall's hue (mount at ceiling line and extend shade 3 to 4 inches past the window's opening or trim, too).
- Station a chair, plant, decorative box, or other piece of furniture in front of tiny windows to distract the eye from the bottom edge of the window and the (seemingly endless) wall space beneath it.

- Camouflage window-unit air conditioners behind wood slat blinds or shutters mounted either outside the window frame for shallow windows or inside-mounted far enough out in a deeper window box recess to clear the unit. Air will still flow with the blinds down and open.
- The easiest way to dress an arched (Palladian) window is to hang curtains above the arch (close to the ceiling—we're on a roll!). Tying the curtains back on either side looks lovely, too, if you're going for a more traditional look. If the arched element is separate, curtaining just the lower part of the window isn't the end of the world (but won't look as good as a single curtain mounted above the arch, baby).
- With windows that are *waaaaaaaaay* up high on a wall (i.e, clerestory, or maybe in a stair hall), you're off the hook!

Hang curtains above the tip top of a Palladian window. *Regal*, dahling!

These look better left bare, so they can flood your room with light during the day (and are so high up that they don't look like gaping black holes at night).

- Waterproof is the way to go for bathroom windows. Faux wood or Durawood slat blinds are just the ticket for mildew-free W.C. chic, as are vinyl shutters or Roman shades made of indoor-outdoor acrylic like Sunbrella. Any of these work even if your in-the-shower window takes a daily drenching every time you do. For damp (and not drenched) spaces that require more colorful options, aluminum blinds are rust-resistant, too. (Make sure they're *pure* aluminum, though—alloys can rust.)

- City dwellers whose landlords have stuck them with nasty steel security gates, take heart! Outside-mounted shutters will hide your visual catastrophe and keep both you *and* your security deposit safe.

- Venture beyond the drapery panel for Roman shades and smaller windows. Shower curtains and sheets can be stylish options, *especially* the irresistibly patterned ones for children's rooms. (And shower curtains are already pre-holed for rings! *J'adore!*)

FLOORING, CARPETING, AND AREA RUGS

They're the foundation of every interior, they set the tone for everything that happens on top of them, and they're the most consistent element of design throughout a house (or at least they *should* be: Wall finishes and window treatments can vary dramatically from room to room, but your flooring rarely should or you'll get dizzy by the third space you hit and wonder if you've (A) floated next door or (B) ventured into a flooring showroom). If you're designing from the ground up (ha ha ha!) and are stymied about what to lay down first,

I'll share a secret with you: Choosing flooring materials can be hard.

The possibilities are endless enough to make you want to do something different in every room . . . and alas! you shouldn't (see above, star pupil). Once you set foot past your home's foyer, flooring isn't where you want to play out your wildest decorating fantasies. (Save *that* for your powder room, sugar!) Fixing a regrettable paint color choice is as easy as rolling out a couple of new coats of paint and will set you back maybe a gallon of matte latex. Fixing an unfortunate *flooring* choice, though, can *bankrupt your decorating budget* (*and* make life miserable for you while you have to wait—double whammy)! So it's one of the very few things decoratively that you want to try to get right the first time. Here are some useful flooring rules of thumb to help you out:

- Choose a material that works with your lifestyle and your household makeup (i.e., animals you live with, including toddlers, pets, teenage boys, your husband . . .).
- The lighter the floor, the larger the room will look, which is the best news *ever* for small spaces. Know that nothing opens up a claustrophobic, closet-size room like a glacier white floor, and then downscale from there to your own level of light-hued practicality (i.e., a lot).
- Dark-stained wood floors look breathtakingly beautiful in magazine spreads (and can be equally drop-dead *gaw-ge-ous chez vous*), but they'll show every speck of dust that hits them (and some that just merely fly by), so if you're allergic to frequent vacuuming and Swiffering (and don't have a handy daily staff taking care of that dreariness for you,

dahling, right after your breakfast in bed and your workout with your personal trainer), then *maaaaaaybe* you'd like to go with a lighter (but still stylishly rich) dark walnut instead.

- It's visually important to contrast the color of your floors with the color of your walls to create visual warmth and depth in a room. Anchor light-hued walls with darker floors, and relieve darker walls with light-colored floors. (Of course, if you're going for a womb-like effect décor-wise, go ahead and *envelope yourself* in total darkness all around, sweetie, and enjoy! *Lighters up!!*)

- If you can't resist the dark floors + deep wall color combo, fashionista that you are, sit your dark-hued furniture on a lighter-colored area rug to get the contrast thing going without losing your dark, gleaming edge.

Whatever look you go for, *do* try to have your flooring vary only slightly in your primary public rooms to maintain style continuity house-wise (i.e., border/borderless, or choosing a more dramatic layout like a herringbone with an inset border for red carpet spaces like dining rooms and libraries). Give your flooring lots of thought—remember that curtains come and go, but that walnut parquet will most likely be around for generations, a lasting memento of your unforgettable style and taste. Be sure to leave a legacy underfoot, baby.

We've talked about lots of flooring options and designs in other chapters (see Kitchens, Chapter 5; and Basements, Chapter 8), so here's a gander at some other great materials:

I. WOOD, NATURAL OR ENGINEERED

Wood flooring, either natural or engineered (man-made), comes in an impressive variety of widths, shapes, colors, and finishes and is by far the most popular flooring choice in America. There's one for your taste and lifestyle, no matter which end of the luxury spectrum you're on.

Solid Wood

Hardwood flooring, laid out in planks, either straight run or in a charming pattern, is, like its name implies, *hard* and durable (as opposed to softer woods like pine, which are cru-

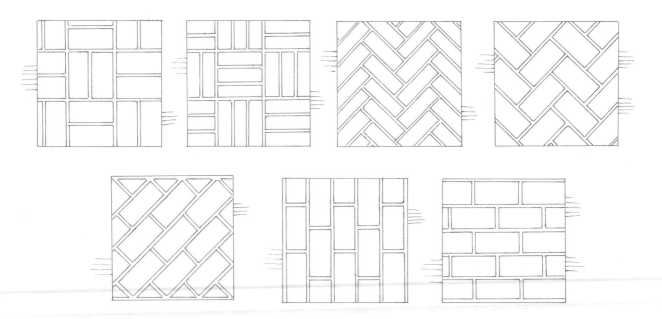

Take inspiration from tile layouts for wood floors, too.

elly wounded by every stiletto and skateboard that grazes them). Easily stained oak is the number one species for most hardwood floors you see, but the list—and their grains—is endless, from mahogany to walnut to wenge, maple to Brazilian cherry and more, from the exotic to the organic to your just-your-average-joe species, all widely available at major home centers everywhere.

Size-wise, planks range from 2¼ inches in width to up to 20 inches wide (but, honey, 20-inch planks look *so* Betsy Ross circa 1776—I *reeeeeally* wouldn't unless you just *haaaaad* to). The wider the plank, the more "antique" the feel (but *do* exercise restraint and stop yourself at about the 6-inch mark, doll; anything wider is really too much of a good thing).

Wood flooring is either new or *reclaimed*, which means that it's more than seventy-five years old (and thus only five years short of being antique!). Reclaimed wood features instant patina, which *might* help you get over its sticker shock, although if you seek you shall surely find more affordable options online (from demolished barns in Maine, for example).

Rule of Thumb

Hardwood swells and buckles when wet (think snow moguls when skiing), so it's not a good option for spaces that regularly are damp and wet. However, it *is* fine for kitchens (wipe up spills pronto) and powder rooms (ditto).

If you're going for the grainless look, there's almost no better choice than maple. It's hard (basketball courts!), virtually grain-free, and looks stunning in its lightness. If you'd like to have a *dark* maple floor, plan on having it *aniline dyed* and not stained, since maple takes stain notoriously unevenly. Aniline dye penetrates all the way through the wood, as opposed to stain, which just colors its uppermost layer and leaves the wood beneath its natural color. If it sounds like a lot more work to dye your floor rather than stain it, that's because it *is*.

While we're at it, here's a review of the standard technique for finishing a wood floor: It's sanded clean to remove any existing finish, two or more coats of stain are applied next (personally, I prefer at least three coats, to *reeeeeeally* get that lavishly rich color you're after; the darkest colors can need up to four, so *insist*!), followed by two coats of a protective finish like polyurethane (three if you live in a shopping mall). If you live in a super-sleek, modern dwelling (and admire the high-sheen, gleaming reflection of, say, a basketball court— *just kidding*!), then high-gloss poly may well be your ticket to shine. Otherwise choose satin finish poly for a more discreet luster that leaves the room's emphasis on what's on top of the floor rather than the floor itself.

Waxed—and not poly'ed—hardwood floors exude an Old World, fine furniture gleam, and I'll confess that they *do* look fabulous. And also that they're high maintenance. A polyurethaned floor can hold up under *years* of regular traffic before it needs refreshing, but your waxed beauty (two or three coats of stain, as usual + two coats of wax, buffed in between) will require yearly stripping and re-waxing to maintain its good looks. Along with regular buffing (weekly if

TRADE SECRET

Get the exact color of stain that your heart desires by mixing two or more stains to create your pleasure. Have your flooring pro (A) immediately write down the percentage combo before he forgets and can't replicate it, and then (B) make a 3 by 3-foot sample on a piece of your sanded floor (and not someone else's that might not take color identically like yours). Do as many samples of color combos that you need to get it right (two or three but not more, to avoid an upcharge for resanding your entire floor after the sampling, hon). ✳

you're anal, monthly if you're not) in between. All of a sudden your floor is the highest maintenance person you know!

Add visual impact to your wood plank floor with a 2- to 4-inch-wide contrast wood border around its perimeter, set in 6 to 8 inches from the outer edge, in either a contrasting-hued hardwood or a cute little pattern (check online for inspiration). Choose more detailed insets for your public spaces (i.e., living room, dining room) and simpler ones for private spaces and halls.

The smaller the space, the narrower the border should be. In square rooms—especially foyers, dining rooms, and powder rooms, a center medallion or other cute little geometric motif like a star adds interest *and* eliminates the need for an area rug. (If you live in Texas, go ahead and succumb to your desire to have your initials inset into the center, sugar, but do it upstairs in a private hall and not in your foyer.)

Engineered Flooring

Engineered or *pre-finished wood flooring* consists of razor-thin sheets of wood glued together to make a plank, then stained and most always polyurethaned by the manufacturer. Some are thick enough to be sanded at least once; most are not (check with the manufacturer to be sure). Available in widths of up to 7 inches, they're designed with a tongue-in-groove base that simply snaps together to put each plank into place, laid out on top of a plastic "membrane" that the flooring manufacturer also fabricates. Engineered wood flooring snaps easily into place over concrete subfloors or preexisting wood floors that can't be refinished. (Don't confuse *engineered flooring* with *laminate flooring*; see Basements, page 161, for more on laminate floors.) And while nothing ever *truly* replicates the style and elegance of genuine hardwood floors, engineered floors come as close as you can get. Like their laminate cousins, they're super-easy to install, already stained to perfection, and you've gotta love the *odorless* convenience of not having to wait twenty-four hours for each coat of poly to dry. Oh, wait—did I forget to mention that they're cheaper than the Real McCoy (unless, of course, you go for the opulent and exotic stuff, bunny)?

Parquet

Manhattan rental apartments are legendary for their (cheesy) parquet flooring. My fellow Manhattanites, *be informed!* The truth is, there's parquet and then *there's parquet* (which NYC landlords aren't inclined to splurge on, alas). Traditional parquet floors are crafted from luxuriously thick blocks of oak, birch, cherry, mahogany, or teak and most commonly arranged in a fancy pattern such as herringbone. Apartment rental parquet is made of bases of plywood or medium density fiberboard (MDF) topped with a thin little strip of hardwood veneer. The good news (*positive thinking!!*) is that most apartment parquet can be refinished at least twice before you hit their end of the refinishing road (not so good if the tenant before you got there first, though!). But back to the good news: If one of your parquet floor tiles is damaged, it can easily be removed and replaced. (And your super probably has a stash of them in the basement.)

If you move into a rental with a dull parquet floor, here's

the reason: Most landlords install it and apply polyurethane over it without staining it. Girlfriend Decorator says to sand it, apply two coats of lavishly hued stain, and top it with two coats of satin poly (*definitely* avoid the high gloss here, honey, along with colors that will make you *lose your security deposit*!).

Bamboo

Bamboo flooring is the It Floor du jour, delightfully green and environmentally friendly. Fast-growing and easily harvested, more building products have been made with bamboo in the last ten years than George Washington Carver made with the peanut ages ago. Bamboo stalks are cut into strips and laminated together to flooring that's as durable as oak and can mimic tons of pretty wood species, either unfinished or factory finished. Bamboo flooring takes stain well and holds up almost as well as oak. It's a great choice for wherever a traditional wood floor would go and is especially simpatico with radiant-floor heat because it doesn't expand or contract the way solid woods do.

CONCRETE AND POURED EPOXY

If you're going after a sleek, modern look, concrete or poured epoxy floors can be just what the doctor ordered—they aren't just for garages and basements anymore! Concrete can be tinted almost any color, followed by an acrylic resin seal once it completely hardens, about a month after it's installed. Poured epoxy flooring is seamless, super-glossy, and a pleasure to walk on. It's poured in a color, so it doesn't require tinting afterward. True to their industrial origins, both are durable finishes . . . that I recommend having a professional install, just to make sure they're brilliantly done the first time 'round.

II. CARPETING AND AREA RUGS

Area rugs help define the seating groups on top of them (see Living Rooms, page 8), add a visual layer of décor that adds *exponentially* to a room's style and warmth, and also help muffle sound (which apartment dwellers know *lots* about). Wall-to-wall carpeting lets you sink your toes into every square inch of your bedroom floor, and also is great to hide unattractive stairs and boring hallways. (Cute stairs and hallways should have runners, instead.) As a rule, the Style Council wants you to go for hardwood flooring throughout your home, but in a pinch, wall-to-wall works, too, *especially* in rentals where you don't own your floors, or for all-around chic-on-the-cheap, since it can be much less pricier a proposition than putting in hardwood.

Most carpet is sold as *broadloom*, which means it typically comes in 12-foot widths (sometimes, but infrequently, a bit wider), sold by the square foot. Carpet for wider wall-to-wall installations is installed in multiple pieces that are "seamed" together with carpet tape on-site during the installation.

TRADE SECRET   Be sure to discuss the location of the seam in larger rooms with your carpet vendor before installation, in order to best hide the seam given the exact furniture plan and traffic flow of the room you're carpeting. ✳

Here's the skinny on carpeting and area rug fibers:

Wool

Wool is the gold standard of area rugs and carpeting—well, truthfully, that would be *silk* or *cashmere*, which are so luscious and luxuriously priced that you should just *call me* if you want to talk about them, and we won't waste everyone else's precious reading time here.

Wool holds its shape and resists dirt better than any other fiber out there over the long run, so it holds up better under traffic and is more easily cleaned once soiled. Pure wool is the priciest of the carpet fiber bunch.

Acrylic

Acrylic fibers closely resemble wool but are cheaper, although they don't hold their shape as well (they're more easily crushed, which is problematic for high-traffic rugs). An acrylic-fiber rug is a fabulous alternative for folks with an allergy to wool.

Nylon

Nylon is one of the most popular, well-priced fibers for carpeting today. It's a strong, resilient (holds its shape, doll), stain-resistant material that wears well and holds up *mahvelously* under lots of traffic, more so than our next entry . . .

Polypropylene

Polypropylene (*olefin*) is another value-priced man-made fiber. It's stain resistant (but not for oil stains), and can melt under extremely hot temperatures or if heavy furniture is vigorously dragged across it (all that friction, natch). We like polypropylene because of its water resistance, which means that it's the material of choice for outdoor area rugs. Olefin is solution dyed (i.e., in its molten state, before it's spun and shaped into a thread) and holds color brilliantly (which the sun won't fade). Know that it crushes easily, however, so don't go looking for it in a pile carpet—stick to the low and the looped.

Polyester

Polyester holds color brilliantly, is attractively priced, and is also stain resistant. It's another good option if you're allergic to wool. Like polypropylene, though, it isn't the most resilient fiber (that would be nylon, darling), and can also crush and squish easily, which could be problematic if the entire Boy Scout troop stomps all over it once a week, fifty-two weeks a year.

Sisal, Sea Grass, Coir, and Jute

The Favored Nation of area rugs for design cognoscenti around the world is hemp. Sisal, sea grass, coir, and jute are woven rugs made from the fiber of the hemp plant (like giant strips of twine—no wonder your cat will adore your sisal rug almost as much as you do!). They're the neutral no-rug rug, and they add texture to and anchor a room stylishly without visually competing with what's on top. Sea grass is considered to be the chicest, for either sisal or wall-to-wall, although jute is easier on bare feet. Clean up any spills or stains on your sisal flooring the *nanosecond* they happen—these rugs are as notoriously *un*-stain-resistant as they are easy on the eye.

COLOR CHEAT SHEET

COLOR MADE SIMPLE!

The number one question I get asked about as a designer is "can you help me understand color?" Well, with forty-two thousand different colors out there under the sun, *of course* trying to pick out TWO for your living room can sometimes seem more intimidating than *raising children*! Not to worry, dolls—your Girlfriend Decorator here has figured it all out for you. Here is everything you need to know to control your color selecting, as opposed to letting *it* control you!

- How to Combine Colors—Here's the only rule you'll ever need to know to figure out if colors go together: If a color combination exists in nature, in a landscape, a flower, or a fruit, it will work in your home. (And in your outfit, too, just in case you were wondering if that sweater went with those pants!) Choose a couple of the strongest colors as your main colors for upholstery, a pretty one you can live with daily for your walls (see more on selecting a wall color, below), and a couple—or more— of the brightest or most unusual hues (i.e., fuchsia) as accents for throw pillows and accessories. Darling, It's! That! Simple!

- This is why turquoise, beige, and cream go together (colors of the beach); red, orange, brown, and green merge marvelously (colors of the autumn field); purple, brown, magenta, and green are sublime (as they are in an eggplant); navy, pink, apricot, cream, and brown look lovely together (as they do in the early evening sky); and violet, navy, and green are adorable (inspired by a hydrangea flower).

- The Color Family Lowdown—Hearing all that talk about *warm, cool, summer, winter,* and *fall* can be confusing. So *fuggedaboudit*! Remember this, and this alone: Colors are divided into either *warm* (the colors of the sun: yellows, oranges, reds, etc.) or *cool* (the colors of water, grass, and the sky: blues, greens, etc.) families. That's all you need to know to be a color genius, and remembering it is as easy as looking up when you're outside!

- How to Choose Colors for Your Rooms—Number one, ask yourself what colors you like best. The easiest way to do this is to start with your wardrobe. Do you wear fashionista black, gray, and beige every day? Or are you an exotic bird of the tropics, luxuriously festooned in bright colors from head to toe? Are you Prada'ed out (including the look for less, dahling) in clean, sculptural silhouettes? Are you ruffled, soft, girly, and chic? Your daily clothing selections (lawyers, bankers, doctors, and Starbucks employees, what are y'all wearing on the *weekends*?) reveal more about your personality than almost anything else, *especially* the design aesthetic that appeals to you most. You'll want something comparable for your home.

TRADE SECRET   Fashion and interior design are a lot alike, except that one dresses bodies and the other dresses rooms. But if you consider that you dress your *rooms* so that your *body* can live in them, you'll see how they really do go together more than you think! (Except that a room doesn't have to worry about hemlines rising and falling every season!) Think about putting a room together just like you put an outfit together and decorating becomes a lot less intimidating and more fun. Put fabrics together just as you would getting dressed, with one color being the star and everything else playing in the supporting cast: You have something that anchors the look (pants = sofa); supporting colors that complement the anchor (shirt = other upholstery pieces such as club chairs); and you finish it with bright, shiny, or unusual items to accent your look (throw pillows and decorative objects = accessories and bijoux—or socks and a tie if you're a guy). Voila! You're dressed for the day and your living room looks *faaaabulous*, too! ✱

- The Four Q's of Choosing a Wall Color—You've heard the "warm colors make a room look smaller; cool colors vice versa" schtick a million times. Honey—as my mother would say—"that's *foolishness.*" (Although there *is* an element of truth to it, I'll confess—but there's *so* much more to the story than that! So we won't obsess.) Here are the four things to consider when choosing a wall color for your room (after you've thought about basic colors you crave):

- *How much sunshine does the room get?* Does your space face south (= a lot of sunshine) or north (= not so much but some in the morning), east (you get the picture). Strong, rich, dark colors look amazing in a sunlight-filled room. On the other hand, you should *avoid* super-bright colors in a super-sunny space, since you'd eventually come to feel like bacon in a frying pan when you're in them. Keeping the brights in your fabrics in those rooms and selecting cool hues—shades of whites, beiges, or pastels, or even luscious darks—for wall colors is a better option for super-bright spaces. However, if you'll simply *die* unless your blindingly bright room is red, orange, or yellow, then choose the richest, deepest versions of those colors, like ochre, mustard yellow (dried mustard, not fresh, sugar), sangria, or deep hunting red. Add brightness to your daytime bat cave by painting your walls rich, warm hues—the brighter the better. Muted colors work well in rooms that get sunshine only part of the day, but be sure to ban the blah with a bouncy fabric here and there (citrus-colored pillows in a taupe or khaki room, for example).

- *How big is the room? How much time will you be spending in there?* The less time you spend in a room, the more outrageous it can be, and vice versa. This is what makes powder rooms the most perfect theaters for drama and shockingly hued walls, no matter what their size. Conversely, you should select more soothing colors that you *adore* for your family room, bedroom, and kitchen, because you're in them twenty-seven hours a day.

- *What time of day will you be using the room, and what are you doing in there?* If you're a workaholic singleton who's never at home during the day, then you want your house to be a knockout by lamplight at night. If you're a stay-at-home mom with three kids underfoot, then your house should look *mahvelous* during daylight hours. Dining rooms used mostly for dinner should look their best at the dinner hour (whatever yours may be). One last thing: You can't make a room look larger with color (the truth is, you can only prevent it from looking any smaller), so if a room is small and dark and you're mostly using it at night, then, lovey, make it smaller and darker (you'll need lots of lamplight, though—I said dark, not dimly lit!), and it will be the coziest room of the house.

- *Who's using the room?* The one rule of design that your Decorator Girlfriend here never breaks is that *rooms should look like the people who live in them.* And that goes for every room of your house, including your kids' rooms, your husband's man cave, your living room, and your foyer. Even. Your. Garage. Because if your house doesn't look like you, then, sugar, you never really get to go home.

• Don't Be a Slave to Fashion When Selecting Colors—Because, baby, repainting a room costs *waaaaaay more* than buying a new pair of shoes. If you *can't resist* submitting to the It Color du jour, then put it in a space that will be easy to have repainted if you tire of it in a couple of years, one where the furniture is easily moved to the center of the room and won't require relocating to a temporary off-site domicile for ages while the work is done. At the end of the day, wall color is just the backdrop against which your lovely things are seen.

- How to Make an All-White Room Work—Texture, texture, texture! Achieving warmth and coziness in a room is about balancing shiny + matte, fuzzy + sleek, patterned + plain, and dark + light in furnishings, textiles, and finishes. Monochromatic rooms need even more of that mix. Be sure to vary your whites a bit: Go from the Ice Station Zebra blinding-blizzard white to a softer ivory and a pale dove white. But vary those textures even more.

- How to Mix Dramatically Colored Rooms Without Your House Looking Like the Circus—When you change wall colors throughout a house, keep the *corridors that join the rooms* as neutral territory, so the diverse colors emanate off of that. Now, don't start thinking *white* when I say *neutral*, bunny—think ivory, beige, gray, khaki, or whatnot—and then use that color *consistently* throughout the entire zone (like all the halls and the stairway). P.S.: Hallways are also a great place for creating faux texture by painting or papering tone-on-tone stripes (use a slightly lighter + slightly darker version of one single color, maybe two colors away on the paint card; 7-inch stripes for the tiniest small spaces, 9-inch-wide ones for the rest).

- Rethink Standard-Issue White Trim—Okay, so it *does* still look good lots of the time, but I want you to *move* beyond Super White. When only white trim will do, check out the softer ivories, grayed whites, and creams. *But:* ALWAYS avoid super white ceilings! They make even the fanciest abodes look like spec houses. Choose a pale café au lait or deepish ivory instead. Have your painter add a little of the wall color to an ivory to get the hue just right. The British have always done the most adorable job at whipping up great-looking nonwhite trim colors, and early Americans (think thirteen colonies and 1776) did a great job, too (obviously still influenced by the motherland!). Check out historic landmark buildings in America online (such as Winterthur in Delaware) and international decorating magazines online or at your newsstand for inspiration. Easier still: Consider making your trim color a couple of shades darker than your wall color, which can look *amazing*. While I'm at it, remember that your ceiling should almost NEVER be the same color as the walls, unless you REALLY know what you're doing and took the A.P. Color Class and passed with *flying colors.*

- Splurge on the Best Paint Job You Can Afford—Buying cheap paint is an exercise in futility. It takes more to cover less, and, adding insult to injury, it'll start off looking merely mediocre and then head from bad to worse as it ages. Buying quality paint is a worthwhile investment in the place you love the most, that also loves you back. I always say: *Great paint jobs can outlast many marriages.* It's better to divide your painting project into affordable phases than to stint on the paint job.

- Here's what you *don't* get when you opt for the budget paint job: The walls are never properly sanded, filled, smoothed, primed, and prepared. If a tiny crack was neglected today, it will grow up into a very big crack later on. And if you turn bright lights on in your room, your walls will look unevenly surfaced and horrendous.

- Test Your Paint Color in the Actual Light of the Room You're Painting—The paint on the swatch is the exact color it will be on your wall (unless it is a thousand-year-old paint swatch and has faded), only there will be a whole lot more of it, so the end result might surprise you. Purchase a test pot of the paint you're considering (buy a quart if it doesn't come in test sizes) and paint a big 3-foot-square patch of the color on your walls (two coats, pookie!), and see how you like it morning, noon, and night.
- Select Sherbet and Citrus for Accent Colors—Just as sherbet is the "universal dessert," tasting great after just about everything, and a little lemon or lime juice goes great with almost anything, sherbet and citrus colors are the universal accent colors for design. There isn't a color scheme out there than couldn't use a little splash of mango, apricot, banana, lemon, tangerine, raspberry, persimmon, pear, or lime in a throw pillow or decorative object. Use common sense when picking from the fruit bowl, though, and take the neighboring colors into consideration, too.

INDEX

Note: Page numbers in *italics* refer to illustrations.
Page numbers followed by a *t* refer to text boxes.

gold-leafed walls, 82–83, 120
granite countertops, 109
great rooms, 1. *See also* living
      spaces
groupings
  in bathrooms, *144*, 144
  of framed pieces,
       25–28, 25*t*, *26*, *27*,
       65–66, *66*
  in laundry rooms, 188
  in odd numbers, 28*t*
  in powder rooms, 82
grout, 135, 136*t*
G-shaped kitchens, 96, *97*
gyms, 158, 161, 174

H

hallways, 4*t*, 236
headboards, *62–63*
heating
  in basements, 168–69
  in bathrooms, 136–37
  in kitchens, 112–13
  and wood flooring, 225
hemp rugs, 228–29
highboys
  in dining rooms, 34, *35*
  in living spaces, 11–13, *12*
high hats. *See* recessed
      lighting
high-performance furniture,
      17–18
honeycomb blinds, 198

horizontal sliding sash windows
      (gliders), 191, *192*
humidifiers, 169*t*

I

industrial rubber floors, 112
insulation, 169
island kitchens, 96, *97*, 98,
      119–20

J

jalousie windows, 191
jute rugs, 228–29

K

kitchens, 91–124
  art in, 111, *123*, 124
  backsplashes, 101, 110–11
  in basements, 158
  cabinets, 99–101, 100*t*, 105–8,
     105*t*, *106*
  countertops, 101–3, 108–9
  details, 119–20
  dishwashers, 98–99, 103
  floors, 111–13, *113*, 221*t*
  laminates, 109, 110, 119
  layout, 92–99, 92–93*t*, *94*, *95*,
     96, *97*
  lighting, 116–18
  range hoods, 114–16
  seating, 104–5

ABOUT THE AUTHOR

New York–based interior designer and recognized tastemaker Elaine Griffin believes that a home should look like the people who live there and like nobody else. "A person's home—what it looks like, where it is, how it's lived in—reveals more about them than absolutely anything else in the world," she says. "I want everyone to take pride in where they live, how *marvelous* it looks, and how perfectly comfortable it feels for them to live there. It doesn't feel like 'home sweet home' until your décor *enhances* your personality, and doesn't ignore or eclipse it."

A graduate of Yale University who studied at the New York School of Interior Design, Elaine began her design career in the office of architectural behemoth Peter Marino following her nine-year career as a publicist in New York and Paris, and officially opened her own firm in 1999.

A native of Georgia, Elaine makes frequent appearances on television and online. Her design advice, projects, and makeovers have been featured in publications including *Elle Decor, The New York Times, Southern Accents, House Beautiful, Better Homes and Gardens, O at Home,* the *New York Post* and New York *Daily News.*

Elaine lives in New York City with her husband and two cats.